Top Down Policymaking

Thomas R. Dye
Florida State University
and
The Lincoln Center for Public Service

CHATHAM HOUSE PUBLISHERS
SEVEN BRIDGES PRESS, LLC
NEW YORK · LONDON

Seven Bridges Press, LLC
135 Fifth Avenue, 9th Floor
New York, NY 10010-7101

Publisher: Ted L. Bolen
Managing Editor: Katharine Miller
Composition: Linda Pawelchak/Lori Clinton
Printing and Binding: Victor Graphics

Library of Congress Cataloging-in-Publication Data

Dye, Thomas R.
    Top down policymaking / Thomas R. Dye
        p. cm.
    Includes index.
    ISBN 1-889119-33-4
    1. Political planning—United States. 2. Elite (Social sciences—United
States. 3.
    Pressure groups—United States. 4. Campaign funds—United States. I. Title.

    JK468.P64 D93 2001
    320'.6'0973—dc21   00-0644379

Manufactured in the United States of America
10 9 8 7 6 5 4 3 2 1

Contents

Tables and Figures

Tables

Preface

TOP DOWN POLICYMAKING provides a thorough evaluation of the processes by which the national elite goes about transforming its own values, interests, and preferences into public policy. It is a study of the way in which public policy is made. It briefly describes the structure of wealth and power in America, but it focuses principally on how wealth and power flow into government and the policymaking process.

Top Down Policymaking sets forth a model of national policymaking that envisions four separate processes by which elites influence the policies of government—the policy formulation process, the interest group process, the leadership selection process, and the opinion making process. It then proceeds to describe government legitimation and implementation of the policy initiatives and reforms inspired by national elites. Finally, it describes both public and private processes of policy evaluation.

This book argues that even in a democracy, public policy is made from the top down, not from the bottom up. It describes how the policy agenda flows downward from elites to government through a network of foundations, "think tanks," policy planning organizations, and the media. It describes the crucial role of monied elites in selecting the nation's political leadership. It describes the elite-financed interest group process that dominates policymaking activity in Washington. And it describes the unique role of the nation's media elite in policy formulation and the communication of elite views to both government decision makers and the masses of Americans.

Policies are given legitimacy by the institutions of government; legitimacy does not arise out of popular support for the policies themselves. Indeed, this book argues that there is a notable lack of congruence between the policy preferences of the American public and current national policies on a number of highly visible issues. It also argues that Congress itself functions largely on the basis of top-down leadership and, moreover, that the costs of running for Congress virtually guarantee the dependency of its members on financial elites.

It argues that the policy implementation process, lodged in the Washington bureaucracy, is closely monitored by the nation's elite both directly and through interest group oversight. And it argues that the most important function of government from the perspective of the nation's elite—the regulation of the money supply—is undertaken independently of any elected officials by the Federal Reserve Board.

Throughout this volume, boxed features focus on relevant topics and key players in the current policymaking environment, offering vivid illustration of the top-down policymaking model. Among the issues highlighted are elite attitudes toward citizen policymaking, global trade policy, preferential tax treatment for investors, the influence of money in politics, tobacco legislation, the conflicting policy views of media and business elites, "banking reform," the divergence of public policy from popular preferences, mass distrust of government bureaucracies, public opinion about government waste, and the evaluation and reform of welfare policy. Among the influential elites profiled are the Ford Foundation, the Council on Foreign Relations and the Trilateral Commission, the Conservative Policy Network, the Business Roundtable, the media empires, and the Federal Reserve Board.

ACKNOWLEDGMENT

Support for research and preparation of this book was provided by the Lincoln Center for Public Service, a nonprofit, nonpartisan education and research organization serving the citizens of Florida and the nation. The views expressed in this book are those of the author only; they do not necessarily represent the views of the Lincoln Center for Public Service, its officers, or its trustees (Lincoln Center for Public Service, Suite 224, Bank of America Center, 1801 South Federal Highway, Delray Beach, Florida, 33483).

CHAPTER 1

Policymaking from the Top Down

The discovery that in all large-scale societies the decisions at any given time are typically in the hands of a small number of people confirms a basic fact: Government is always government by the few, whether in the name of the few, the one, or the many.

—HAROLD LASSWELL

PUBLIC POLICY IN America, as in all nations, reflects the values, interests, and preferences of the governing elite. The assertion that public policy reflects the "demands of the people" expresses the myth rather than the reality of democracy. However widespread this myth is believed by the people, and however artfully this myth is defended by scholars, the reality is that *public policy is made from the top down.*

To say that public policy in a democratic society is made from the top down is not to disparage democracy. The underlying values of democracy—liberty and equality—define individual dignity. These are fundamental moral values, not granted by governments, but belonging to every individual as a matter of natural right. And government by the consent of the governed—with free, periodic, competitive elections in which each person's vote is equal to that of every other person—defines the minimal processes of democracy.

Yet power is unequally distributed in all societies. No government can promise its citizens effective participation in all of the decisions that affect their lives. At most in the United States, only a few thousand individuals have any direct influence over public policy. Even the most ardent defenders of American democracy do not claim that the nation's 275 million people can be brought together to make national decisions: "People could be born, grow old, and die while they waited for such an assembly to make one decision."[1] The Founders of the nation never even considered including national referenda voting in the U.S. Constitution.

Power in American society is concentrated in the hands of the relatively few people who control its largest organizations and institutions. These are the people who make policy for the nation; they are the "national elite." Even in a democracy, "the immediate or proximate decision makers in government, in business, and in the nonprofit sector comprise a small fraction of the citizenry. . . . So, troubling as it may be, the existence of a decision-making elite—or, more accurately, elites—is a fact of political life."[2]

Top Down Policymaking is a study of the process by which power is exercised in America. The policymaking process refers to the way in which public policy is made. It does not refer directly to the composition of the national elite—that is, who really decides policy issues—although this book briefly describes the structure of wealth and power in America. Nor does this term refer directly to the outcomes of the process—that is, the activities of government in social welfare, health care, national defense, education, environmental protection, and so on—although this book introduces various substantive policy issues as illustrations. Rather, *Top Down Policymaking* focuses on how policies are made.

WHAT IS PUBLIC POLICY?

Public policy is whatever governments choose to do or not to do.[3] This simple definition contrasts with the frequent assumption that a "policy" must be a continuing series of activities with a goal, objective, or purpose. But the problem raised in assuming that government actions must have goals in order to be labeled "policy" is that we can never be sure whether or not any particular action has a goal, or if it does, what that goal is. However much we may wish that governments act in a "purposeful, goal-oriented" fashion, we know that in reality they frequently do not do so. Our simple definition—*public policy is whatever governments choose to do or not to do*—includes not only government action but also government inaction. Government failure to act also constitutes policy. Government inaction may have just as great an impact on society as government action.

Top-down policymaking does not necessarily imply the oppression or exploitation of the masses of people. National elites may act out of narrow, self-serving interests or enlightened "public regarding" motives. They may choose to initiate reforms in the interests of mass well-being, occasionally even at some expense to themselves. They may be motivated to do so by a sense of altruism, or more likely by a sense of enlightened self-preservation. That is, national elites may undertake popular reforms to preserve the existing system and their place in it, to ensure mass support for it, and to avoid mass unrest.

Top-down policymaking recognizes that policies may change over time, but they do so in response to redefinitions by elites of their own interests and preferences. The top-down view of policymaking does not imply the absence of social change; it is not a static view of public policy. It is true that national elites are generally conservative, in the sense that they wish to preserve the existing economic and political system and their dominant position in it. But America's national leadership understands the need for continuing modifications in public policy to keep abreast of economic, technological, and even social change. They understand the need for a responsive policy process. But they prefer that changes be incremental rather than revolutionary, that policies be modified rather than replaced.

WHO'S ON TOP?

Power and wealth in America are concentrated in large institutions. The nation's elite are those individuals who occupy positions of authority in institutions that allocate society's resources—that is, those individuals who decide who gets what.

The institutional basis of power in modern society was best described by sociologist C. Wright Mills a half century ago:

> No one . . . can be truly powerful unless he has access to the command of major institutions, for it is over these institutional means of power that the truly powerful are, in the first instance, powerful.   .
>
> If we took the one hundred most powerful men in America, the one hundred wealthiest, and the one hundred most celebrated away from the institutional positions they now occupy, away from their resources of men and women and money, away from the media of mass communication . . . then they would be powerless and poor and uncelebrated. For power is not of a man. Wealth does not center in the person of the wealthy. Celebrity is not inherent in any personality. To be celebrated, to be wealthy, to have power, requires access to major institutions, for the institutional positions men occupy determine in large part their chances to have and to hold these valued experiences.[4]

The national elite is composed of those individuals who formulate, manage, and direct the policies and activities of governments, corporations, banks, insurance and investment companies, mass media corporations, prestigious law firms, major foundations and universities, and influential civic and cultural organizations.[5] Admittedly, there is some autonomy and specialization among leaders in various institutional sectors of American society, some differentiation in spheres of influence, and even some rivalry and competition for preeminence among national leaders.[6] But there is more than enough interaction, linkage, and communication to justify reference to a national elite. And bargaining, accommodation, and compromise are more prevalent than conflict among national leaders. Differences may arise among leaders over the means of achieving common interests, but consensus prevails over the ends of public policy.

Chapter 2 briefly describes the institutional structure of American society and provides a portrait of "the national elite." It describes "who's on top" in the top-down policymaking process. But most efforts are devoted to describing *how* policy is made from the top down.

THE TOP-DOWN POLICYMAKING MODEL

The top-down policymaking model describes the processes by which the national elite goes about transforming its own values, interests, and preferences into public policy. For purposes of analysis we can think of these processes as separate paths by which policy flows from the top down (see figure 1.1). But we should remember that while there is some separation in these processes, and some functional specialization of the key institutions involved in each process, all of them tend to be intertwined. Elite policy preferences are simultaneously communicated through each process.

The Policy Formulation Process

Policymaking begins by deciding what will be the decided. Defining the problems of society—agenda setting—is the first and most important stage of the top-down policymaking process. Conditions in society that are not identified as "problems" never become policy "issues," never become "news," never gain the attention of government officials. Deciding what will be the problem is even more important than deciding what will be the solution.

Agenda setting begins in the boardrooms of banks and corporations, in the lounges of law firms and investment houses, in the editorial conference rooms of media giants, in the meetings of foundation and think tank trustees. Problems are identified and alternative solutions discussed. Powerful people begin to think about societal problems and what, if anything, should be done about them. Multiple corporate, professional, and social contacts among elites encourage the development of agreement about what conditions deserve national attention.

Policy formulation begins when the concerns of elites are communicated to foundations, think tanks, and policy planning organizations. Elites serve on the governing boards of the foundations that provide the financial resources to undertake policy studies, for example, the Ford, Rockefeller, Carnegie, Sloan, Scaife, Mellon, Bradley, Lilly, and Olin Foundations (see chapter 3). These foundations provide the financial support for the think tanks and policy planning organizations that are charged with responsibility to study policy issues and devise solutions, for example, the Council on Foreign Relations, Brookings Institution, Heritage Foundation, American Enterprise Institute, Hoover Institute, and others (see chapter 3). The goals of these foundations and policy planning organizations are to identify policy problems, assemble relevant information, devise policy alternatives, and occasionally even bring together top elites to help develop a consensus about what should be done.

The Leadership Selection Process

Money drives electoral politics in America. No one can seriously contend for a seat in Congress or the desk in the Oval Office without access to money—lots

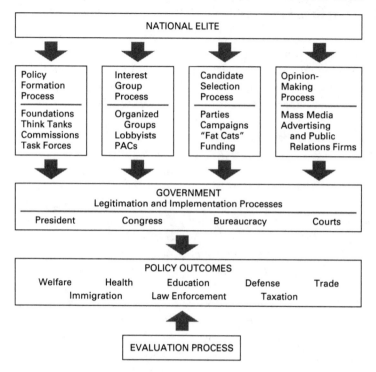

Figure 1.1   Top-Down Policymaking

of it. The costs of campaigning rise dramatically each electoral cycle. The average House member must now raise and spend almost $1 million every two years. U.S. senators must be prepared to raise more than $5, $10, or $25 million every six years. More than $1 billion was spent by all congressional and presidential candidates in the 2000 election cycle.

Where does all this money come from? It comes from the same corporations, banks, insurance companies, law and investment firms, media conglomerates, and wealthy individuals that compose America's national elite. Big money flows through a myriad of party organizations, political action committees, and independent organizations, as well as candidate campaign treasuries (see chapter 4).

Prudent politicians contact moneyed elites *before* deciding to run for office. They try to reassure potential contributors that they share their goals and values, that if elected they will be available to give a sympathetic hearing to their concerns, that they will make every effort in office to accommodate the interests of their contributors, and that they hope their proven loyalty will inspire continued financial support in future elections. A lukewarm response from moneyed elites to early appeals for campaign contributions is a clear signal that a would-be candidate should seek other employment.

The Interest Group Process

The interest group process provides direct support for the policy preferences of elites. Interest groups are organizations that seek to influence government policy—to obtain special benefits, subsidies, privileges, and protections—for their sponsors. They are financed by, and responsible to, the same corporate, banking, financial, professional, legal, media, and civic institutions that compose the national elite.

Washington is a labyrinth of special interest organizations—business, professional, and trade associations; lawyers and law firms; representatives of large corporations; lobbyists and consultants; public and governmental relations firms; and political action committees (see chapter 5). Their lobbying activities are as varied as the imagination of the lobbyists themselves. "Opening doors," establishing personal contacts, "rubbing elbows," and partying and "schmoozing" with government officials are designed to gain access—"just a chance to talk." Lobbying goes well beyond testifying at congressional hearings, contacting government officials, presenting technical information and reports, keeping informed about bills, and following the "ins and outs" of the legislative process. It includes "grass-roots" mobilization of campaign contributors and voters back home, as well as public relations activities designed to develop and maintain a favorable climate of opinion in the nation.

But most important, the special-interest process includes the distribution of campaign funds to elected officials. Campaign contributions from interest groups go overwhelmingly to incumbent officeholders. Vote buying, of course, is illegal. Experienced lobbyists avoid offering a campaign contribution in exchange for a specific favor. But experienced legislators know what to do to keep the campaign contributions flowing.

The Opinion Making Process

The nation's media elites play a dual role in top-down policymaking. The leadership of the mass media is itself a key component of the nation's elite, equal in power to top corporate, banking, insurance, investment, and government elites. But the media elites also perform the crucial function of communicating elite views to government decision makers and to the American public. The media's principal source of power is in communicating the policy agenda—telling elected officials what problems or issues they must address, and telling their mass audiences what should concern them. The mass media is not always successful in telling people what to think, but it is stunningly successful in telling them what to think *about*.

Media power is highly concentrated in the leading television networks (ABC, NBC, CBS, CNN) and the prestigious national press (*New York Times, Washington Post, Wall Street Journal, Newsweek, Time, U.S. News & World Report*).

Media empires are emerging (Viacom, Walt Disney, Time-Warner, etc.) that extend their control from television networks, newspapers, and magazines, to motion pictures, recorded music, sports, and entertainment (see chapter 6).

Policy Legitimation by Government

Policy legitimation is the function of government decision makers—Congress, the president, and the courts. These are the "proximate policymakers." Their activities occur in the final phases of top-down policymaking, well after the agenda for policymaking has been established, policy directions have been formulated, leaders have been selected, interest groups have been activated, and the mass media have brought the issues to their attention (see chapter 7).

Proximate policymaking is the open, public phase of the process. It attracts the attention of most scholars, commentators, and political scientists. And because this phase of the policymaking process involves bargaining and logrolling, persuasion and compromise, competition among interest groups, career enhancement and political credit-taking among elected officeholders, many scholars conclude that these activities characterize the whole of the policymaking process. It is true, of course, that conflict, competition, bargaining, and compromise take place between Congress and the president, between Democrats and Republicans, and between liberals and conservatives. And it is true that the details of the policies that emerge from the governmental process are decided in congressional committees; in the offices and hallways of the Capitol; in discussions among interest group leaders, members of Congress, and their staffs; in executive departments and agencies; and in the White House itself. Finally, it is true that the proximate policymakers are ultimately accountable to the electorate, although these officials have very little confidence in the judgment of their constituents (see feature: "Elite Attitudes toward Citizen Policymaking," pp. 8–9).

But the agenda for policy consideration has been set *before* the proximate policymakers become actively involved in the process, the major directions of policy change have been determined, and the mass media have prepared the public and its representatives for policy action. The decisions which emerge from the formal lawmaking process are not unimportant: who gets the political credit, what agencies get control of the program, exactly how much money will be spent. But these decisions of the proximate policymakers center on the *means* rather than the *ends* of public policy.

Policy Implementation by Bureaucracies

The policy process does not end with the passage of a law by Congress and its signing by the president. Rather, policymaking moves on to the implementation phase—to the departments and agencies of the executive branch of government charged with carrying out policy. Bureaucrats shape policy themselves (see

FEATURE: ELITE ATTITUDES TOWARD CITIZEN POLICYMAKING

More than 200 years ago the British parliamentarian Edmund Burke told his Bristol constituents what he thought about his role as legislator in relation to their policy preferences:

> Certainly, gentlemen, it ought to be the happiness and the glory of a representative to live in the strictest union, the closest correspondence, and the most unreserved communication with his constituents. . . . But his unbiased opinion, his mature judgment, his enlightened conscience, he ought not to sacrifice to you, to any man, or to any set of men living. . . . Your representative owes you, not his industry only, but his judgment; and he betrays you instead of serving you, if he sacrifices it to your opinion.[a]

In our own country Alexander Hamilton may have been the last national leader to publicly acknowledge what elites actually think about the judgment of the masses:

> All societies divide themselves into the few and the many. The first are the rich and the well-born; the other the masses of people. And however often it is said that the voice of the people is the voice of God, it is not true in fact. The people are forever turbulent and changing; they seldom judge right.[b]

The rhetoric of democracy is so ingrained in American political culture that today's leaders instinctively recite democratic phrases. It is extremely difficult to learn their true opinion about the "wisdom of the people." But consider the following response obtained in a special survey of Washington elites:[c]

Do you think the American public knows enough about the issues you face to form wise opinions about what should be done about these issues, or not?

	CONGRESS MEMBERS	PRESIDENTIAL STAFF	SENIOR EXECUTIVE
Yes	31	13	14
No	47	77	81
Maybe	17	7	3
Don't know	5	3	2

Note that fewer than one-third of Congress members believe that the American people know enough to form wise opinions on public issues. Nonelected elites—White House staff and senior executives—have even less confidence in the wisdom of the people. More than three-quarters of them do not believe that the American public can form wise opinions on public issues.

a. A speech to his constituency in Bristol, England, by the Rt. Hon. Edmund Burke, M.P., 1774.

b. Alexander Hamilton, as recorded by James Madison, *Records of the Federal Convention of 1787*.

c. Pew Research Center, as reported in *The Polling Report*, 4 May 1998.

chapter 8). Much of the policymaking process takes place *within* the Office of Management and Budget, the Federal Reserve Board, the Environmental Protection Agency, the Equal Employment Opportunity Commission, the Internal Revenue Service, and hundreds of other bureaucratic centers of power.

The bureaucracy is not constitutionally empowered to make policy, but it does so nonetheless in the policy implementation process. Indeed, as society has grown in size and complexity, the bureaucracy has gained power. It is no longer possible, if it ever was, for Congress or the president to actually govern society. The bureaucracy must assign responsibilities to existing organizations or create new ones, translate laws into operational rules and regulations, hire personnel, draw up contracts, and perform the tasks of governance. All of these activities involve decisions by bureaucrats—decisions that determine policy.

But the bureaucracy is continually monitored by organized interest groups seeking to ensure that policies of the national elite are not significantly altered in the implementation process. And Congress itself spends a great deal of time in bureaucratic "oversight"—trying to ensure that the intent of its laws is reflected in the activities of the bureaucrats.

The Policy Evaluation Process

Elites receive feedback regarding the effects of government policies along the same paths outlined in our top-down policymaking model (see figure 1.1, p. 5). The policy evaluation process is finding out about the effects, if any, of public policy. It is determining whether these effects are those intended and whether the effects are worth the costs of the policy. Governments themselves sometimes undertake policy evaluation. But top-down policy evaluation occurs when elites themselves directly discern policy effects from the information they receive from the institutions they themselves control; or when they receive reports about the effectiveness of government policies from the interest groups, think tanks, and foundations they sponsor; or when the mass media reports on policy effective-ness, or more likely its ineffectiveness, waste, inefficiency, or corruption (see chapter 9).

THE BOTTOM-UP POLICY PROCESS MODEL

The top-down policy model stands in sharp contrast to traditional descriptions of the policymaking process. The prevailing model of policymaking in Ameri-can political science is a popularly driven, "bottom-up" portrait of decision making. This "democratic-pluralist" model assumes that in an open society such as ours any problem can be identified by individuals or groups and brought into the political process for discussion, debate, and resolution. Citizens can define their own interests, organize themselves, persuade others to support their cause, gain access to government officials, influence decision making, and watch over the implementation of government policies and programs.

A variety of democratic institutions are said to facilitate this upward flow of citizen influence. Interest groups, political parties, candidates seeking election to office, and the mass media are all portrayed as responding to popular concerns (see figure 1.2).

Most Americans are skeptical of the bottom-up process. They do *not* believe that the government pays much attention to their policy views or that it under-stands their problems very well. They believe that "the government is run by a

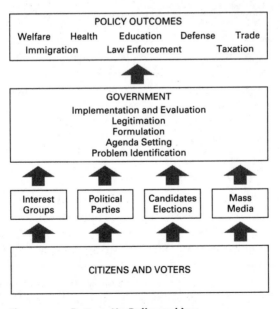

Figure 1.2   Bottom-Up Policymaking

few big interests looking out for themselves." And they believe that members of Congress should pay more attention to public opinion polls (see feature: "Citizen Attitudes toward Elite Policymaking," pp. 12–13). Nevertheless, we want to briefly describe the bottom-up model for the purposes of comparing it with the top-down model.

In the bottom-up model *interest groups* are said to function as important intermediaries between individuals and their government. They supplement the electoral system by providing individuals with the means to directly influence government policy. Organized interest groups act on behalf of individuals in lobbying, testifying at congressional hearings, contacting government officials, overseeing the progress of legislation as well as its implementation by executive agencies, and helping to direct the flow of campaign contributions to responsive public officials.

Political parties are said to be essential for organizing popular majorities to exercise control over government. In theory, "responsible" parties adopt a platform setting forth principles and policy positions; recruit candidates for public office who agree with these principles and policies; inform and educate the voters about public issues; organize and direct campaigns based on principles and issues; and then, after winning control of government, organize the legislature in order to ensure that their policies will be enacted. Of course, in practice it is widely recognized that parties seldom act in this "responsible" fashion. Rather than organize voters around principles or policies, parties seek primarily to win public office. Yet in doing so, it is argued that parties seek to find and express majority opinion. Thus, parties provide yet another means by which popular opinion can be transformed into public policy.

Competitive elections lie at the heart of the democratic process. But in order to transform citizen demands into public policy through elections, several conditions must prevail: candidates must offer of the voters clear policy alternatives, the voters must cast their ballot based on their policy preferences, the outcome of the election must reflect a "policy mandate," and winning candidates must proceed to enact the policies upon which they campaigned. While it is widely acknowledged that these conditions are seldom met in full, nonetheless, voters do tend to favor candidates whose expressed policy views match their own.

The *mass media* themselves reinforce the traditional "bottom-up" model of the policy process by insisting that they merely present a "mirror" of society in their reporting. That is, the media assert that they play an important yet passive role in policymaking—investigating and reporting on the concerns and problems of individual Americans. Media elites generally deny that they have an active role in agenda setting—that is, deciding themselves what problems and issues will receive public attention. Rather they prefer to portray their reporting as a mirroring of popular concerns and issues.

FEATURE: CITIZEN ATTITUDES TOWARD ELITE POLICYMAKING

Should elites make policy according to their own judgment about what is best for America? Or should the views of the majority of citizens prevail in policymaking? This age-old *normative* question about policymaking has taken on new significance in recent decades with the dramatic decline in the American public's trust and confidence in their national leaders. (Chapter 7 examines this decline in greater detail.)

Recent national public opinion polls indicate the following:

Most Americans believe that the government pays very little attention to their views on public policy and that people in government have little understanding of popular thinking.

Over the years, how much attention do you feel the government pays to what the people think when it decides what to do: a good deal, some, or not much?

A good deal	7%
Some	36
Not much	54
Don't know	3

In general, do you think people in government understand what people like you think very well, somewhat well, not that well, or not well at all? (Asked of half the sample)

Very well	2%
Somewhat well	27
Not that well	33
Not well at all	35
Don't know	3

An overwhelming majority of Americans believe that their government is "run by a few big interests looking out for themselves" rather than "for the benefit of all the people."

Would you say the government is pretty much run by a few big interests looking out for themselves, or that it is run for the benefit of all the people?

A few big interests	75%
Benefit of all the people	19
Don't know	7

An overwhelming majority believe that the nation would be better off if public policy followed the views of citizens more closely.

If the leaders of the nation followed the views of the public more closely, do you think the nation would be better off, or worse off than it is today? (Asked of half the sample)

Better	81%
Worse	10
Don't know	10

While elites frequently express disdain for public opinion polls, most Americans believe that policymakers should pay *more* attention to them.

I'm going to read you two statements. Please tell me which statement you agree with most.

(A) *When members of Congress are thinking about how to vote on an issue, they should read up on polls on the issue, because this can help them get a sense of the public's views on the issue.*

(B) *When members of Congress are thinking about how to vote on an issue, they should not read up on polls, because this will distract them from thinking about what they think is right.*

Read polls to sense public's views	67%
Don't read polls, do what you think right	26
Don't know	7

In short, most Americans believe that policy is made from the top down, even though they would prefer more bottom-up policymaking.[a]

a. Center on Policy Attitudes, as reported in *The Polling Report*, 15 February 1999.

The traditional bottom-up model assumes that the most important policymaking activities occur within government itself. Governmental bodies—the president and White House staff, congressional committees and their staff, executive departments and agencies, and the courts—respond to pressures placed on them by organized interest groups, party leaders, electoral politics, and media reporting, in their policymaking activities.

The policymaking process in government is usually represented as a series of activities:

- The *identification* of policy problems through demands for government action
- *Agenda setting,* or focusing the attention of the mass media and public officials on specific public problems to decide what will be decided
- The *formulation* of policy proposals through their initiation and development by policy-planning organizations, interest groups government bureaucracies, and the president and Congress
- The *legitimation* of policies through political actions by parties, interest groups, the president, and Congress
- The *implementation* of policies through organized bureaucracies, public expenditures, and the activities of executive agencies
- The *evaluation* of policies by government agencies themselves, outside consultants, the press, and the public

In short the traditional model views the policymaking process as a series of activities—problem identification, agenda setting, formulation, legitimation, implementation, and evaluation—that take place largely within government.

DEMOCRACY FROM THE TOP DOWN

Top Down Policymaking is not presented as a recommendation or prescription for America. Rather it is presented as an analytic model to help understand and explain the realities of political life in a democracy.

We may all prefer to live in a society where everyone has an equal voice in policymaking; where many separate interests offer solutions to public problems; where discussion, debate, and decision are open and accessible to all; where parties and candidates focus their attention on key public policy issues; where the mass media conscientiously strive to inform and educate citizens and voters about public policy; where policy choices are made democratically; where implementation is reasonable, fair, and compassionate. But although we may prefer such a policymaking process, we nonetheless should strive to understand a more realistic "top-down" system.

Policymaking from the top down is not incompatible with democracy. The central values of American democracy—individual liberty, private property, and equality of opportunity—are not necessarily threatened by top-down decision making. A national elite that is truly limited in its power, bound by constitutional prohibitions against infringement of basic liberties, can rightly claim to be a democratic elite. Its claim is also justified by constitutional arrangements that implement the principle of "government by the consent of the governed"— that is, open, free, periodic, and competitive elections that allow popular majorities to oust governmental leaders.

The nation's Founders—those fifty-five delegates who came together in Philadelphia in 1787 to write the U.S. Constitution—preferred the term "republic" over the term "democracy." They agreed that the origin of government was an implied contract among the people. They believed that the legitimacy of government rested on this contract, that is, on the consent of the governed, not on force. They expected the people to consent to be governed by persons of principle and property, out of recognition of their abilities, talents, education, leadership qualities, and stake in the preservation of ordered liberty.

The Founders believed in a "natural aristocracy." They believed that all people were equally entitled to respect of their natural rights to life, liberty, and property. (Most of the Founders were even aware that this belief ran contrary to the institution of slavery, although they chose to ignore this contradiction.) But for the Founders "equality" did not mean that people were equal in intelligence, talent, wealth, or virtue. They accepted inequalities of wealth and power as a natural product of human diversity. Indeed, they looked upon governmental efforts to force reductions in inequalities as violations of fundamental liberties. In short, the Founders were quite comfortable with the notion of a *national elite*. So are we.

Top Down Policymaking begins with a brief description of the structure of wealth and power in America today (chapter 2). It then proceeds to describe a top-down model of policymaking that challenges the prevailing democratic-pluralist "bottom-up" model, first with respect to policy formulation (chapter 3); and then with respect to the selection of political leadership (chapter 4); the activities of interest groups in Washington (chapter 5); and the role of the mass media in shaping the political agenda and public opinion (chapter 6). It then goes on to describe the more familiar activities of policy legitimation, notably in Congress, but it does so from the perspective of the top-down policymaking model (chapter 7). It observes that the policymaking process continues in the bureaucracy as it goes about the tasks of policy implementation (chapter 8). Finally, *Top Down Policymaking* describes how policies are evaluated by national leaders, both within and outside the government, and how changes and reforms come about. Throughout the book illustrative features are provided to assist in understanding the utility of our top-down policymaking model.

CHAPTER 2

Power, Wealth, and Policymaking

Organized power exists—always and everywhere, in societies large and small, primitive and modern—because it performs the necessary function of establishing and maintaining the version of order by which a given society in a given time and place lives.

—ROBERT LYND

POLICYMAKING IN AMERICA, as in all nations, takes place within society's structure of power and wealth. And power and wealth in America are concentrated in large institutions—industrial corporations, banks, insurance companies, investment firms, media conglomerates, prestigious law firms, and heavily endowed foundations. The institutional organization of society largely determines what issues will be addressed by government and what issues will be systematically organized out of the political system.

Policymakers, like all of us, are affected by the distribution of wealth and income in society, by the structure of institutional power, and by the stratification of social position. Government decision makers, from the president and White House staff and members of Congress and the judiciary, to bureaucrats, administrators, and public employees, all function within the larger stratified society. Like everyone else, they seek to maintain and enhance their own power, wealth, status, and lifestyle.

The institutional structure of society has even more far-reaching effects on policymaking, in its ability to determine what issues will be decided and what issues will never become issues at all. Societal conditions that are never identified as "problems" never become "news," never become "issues," and so do not come to government to resolve. This "non–decision making" occurs when the institutional structure of power and wealth limits the scope of public controversies, even when there may be serious latent problems in society.

Many of the most important determinants of "who gets what" in America lie outside the recognized scope of government, that is, they are considered *private* rather than *public* matters. The decisions of industrial corporations to raise or lower prices or hire or fire workers, of banks to raise or lower interest rates or limit or expand credit, of the mass media to determine what is news, of foundations to decide what research projects shall be funded—all affect our lives as much as do *public* decisions by government.

Even the distribution of wealth and income in America is generally considered a *private* concern. Government may be called on to set an income "floor" below which no one should live; but government does not decide on income ceilings. Thus, government in America does not address itself to inequalities of wealth and income. Yet certainly inequality is a condition which many observers might label a "problem" or "issue." James Madison once observed that "the most common and durable source of faction has been the various and unequal distribution of property. Those who hold and those who are without property have ever formed distinct interests in society."[1]

THE CONCENTRATION OF ECONOMIC POWER

Economic power in America is highly concentrated. Large economic and financial institutions decide what will be produced in the United States and increasingly what will be produced outside it. They decide how many people will be employed and what their wages will be. They determine how goods and services will be distributed and what new products will be developed. They decide how much money will be available for capital investment and where these investments will be made. Decisions made in the boardrooms of these institutions affect our lives as much as those typically made by governments.

Industrial Corporations

The nation's elite includes the relatively small number of senior officers and directors of the nation's largest corporate institutions. Economic power in America is increasingly consolidated in a small number of giant corporations. Indeed, while there are more than 200,000 industrial corporations operating in United States, the fifty corporations listed in table 2.1 (p. 18) control more than 60 percent of all industrial assets in the nation. Typically, the officers and directors of these corporations number between twelve and fifteen; these include the "inside" officer-directors, including the chief executive officer (CEO), as well as "outside" directors who are chosen by the inside directors and the banks and financial institutions that control large blocks of stock in the corporation.

Financial Institutions

The nation's elite also includes the top officers and directors of the nation's commercial banks, insurance companies, and investment firms. The concentration of financial assets in America is even greater than the concentration of the assets of industrial corporations. There are more than 12,000 banks serving the nation, but the twenty-four banks listed in table 2.2 (p. 19) control more than

Table 2.1   America's Largest Nonfinancial Corporations

1. General Motors	26. Kroger
2. Ford Motor	27. Merck
3. Wal-Mart	28. Chevron
4. Exxon	29. Intel
5. General Electric	30. Lockheed Martin
6. International Business Machines (IBM)	31. United Technologies
7. Philip Morris	32. GTE
8. Boeing	33. United Parcel Service
9. AT&T	34. USX
10. Mobil	35. Safeway
11. Hewlett-Packard	36. Costco
12. Sears, Roebuck	37. Conagra
13. DuPont	38. Johnson & Johnson
14. Proctor & Gamble	39. BellSouth
15. KMart	40. Walt Disney
16. Texaco	41. Pepsico
17. Bell Atlantic	42. Ingram Micro
18. Enron	43. Caterpillar
19. Compaq Computer	44. McKesson
20. Dayton Hudson	45. Xerox
21. J.C. Penney	46. Sara Lee
22. Home Depot	47. PG&E
23. Lucent Technologies	48. Raytheon
24. Motorola	49. International Paper
25. SBC Communication	50. Coca-Cola

Source: Derived from data provided in *Fortune,* 26 April 1999.

Note: Ranked by annual revenue. Banking, insurance, investment firms separately ranked.

half of all the banking assets in the United States. Moreover, every year giant new bank mergers are announced: in 1998 Citicorp announced its merger with the Travelers Group (the nation's largest diversified financial institution); BankAmerica merged with NationsBank; and Banc One merged with First Chicago.

While more than 2,000 insurance companies operate in the United States, more than half of all insurance assets in the nation are controlled by the companies listed in table 2.3. Indeed, just two companies (Prudential and Metropolitan) control nearly 30 percent of all insurance assets.

In the field of investment banking, mergers have whittled down the total number of top firms to those listed in table 2.4 (p. 20). These firms decide whether, when, and under what terms corporations can sell stocks, bonds, and other securities. And in recent years, these financial institutions have increasingly

Table 2.2   America's Largest Commercial Banks

1. Citigroup[a]	13. Keygroup
2. BankAmerica	14. Wachovia
3. Chase Manhattan	15. Mellon Bank Corp.
4. First Union	16. Bank of New York
5. Wells Fargo	17. MBNA
6. J.P. Morgan	18. State Street Corp.
7. Bankers Trust	19. Republic New York
8. Fleet Financial	20. Firstar Corp.
9. National City Corp.	21. Comerica
10. PNC Bank	22. Regions Financial
11. U.S. Bancorp	23. BB&T Corp.
12. Suntrust	24. Southtrust

Source: Derived from data provided in *Fortune,* 26 April 1999.

a. Includes merged Travelers Insurance.

Note: Ranked by revenues.

Table 2.3   America's Largest Insurance Companies

Life

1. Prudential	6. American General
2. Metropolitan Life	7. John Hancock
3. New York Life	8. Guardian Life
4. Northwestern Mutual	9. AFLAC
5. Massachusetts Mutual	10. Transamerica

Property

1. State Farm	6. Berkshire Hathaway
2. American International	7. Liberty Mutual
3. Allstate	8. Nationwide
4. Loews	9. St. Paul
5. Hartford	10. Safeco

Health

1. Cigna	6. Tenet
2. Aetna	7. Pacificare
3. Columbia/HCA	8. Foundation
4. United Healthcare	9. Medpartners
5. Humana	10. Wellpoint

Source: Data derived from *Fortune,* 26 April 1999.

Table 2.4 America's Largest Investment Firms

1. Merrill Lynch
2. Morgan Stanley Dean Witter
3. Lehman Brothers
4. Bear Stearns
5. Paine Webber
6. Charles Schwab
7. A.G. Edwards

Source: Data derived from *Fortune*, 26 April 1999.

undertaken to challenge the traditional dominance of "inside" directors of industrial corporations for control of decision making. As holders of the largest blocks of stock in industrial corporations, these institutions are today taking a much more aggressive role in corporate governance. According to *Fortune* magazine: "The fact is, the institutions' fingers are on the most celebrated CEO ousters."[2]

Congress passed the most important financial legislation since the Great Depression in 1999—the Financial Services Act. This law paves the way for banks, insurance companies, and investment firms to merge into colossal mega-corporations. The act repeals the 1933 Glass-Steagall law that was designed to protect bank depositors and insurance buyers from high-risk manipulation of their funds by banks and insurance companies. Glass-Steagall prevented the various types of financial institutions from intermingling funds and services. But after years of interelite squabbles between banks, insurance companies, and investment firms, and after tens of millions of dollars spent on congressional lobbying (see feature: "There's Big Money in Banking," pp. 100–102), Congress opened the door to the creation of all-purpose giant financial mega-firms.

THE GLOBALIZATION OF ECONOMIC POWER

Today, almost one-quarter of the world's total economic output is sold in a country other than one in which it was produced. The United States currently exports about 11 percent of the value of its gross domestic product (GDP) and imports about 12 percent. Exports and imports were only about 3 percent of GDP as recently as 1970.[3]

Historically, America's corporate and financial elite supported high tariffs in order to protect its domestic marketplace. Tariffs on foreign imports forced up their prices and gave U.S. firms sheltered markets. Not only did this improve the profit margins of U.S. corporations, but also it allowed them to operate less efficiently: management became top heavy; its products, especially automobiles, were frequently poor in quality; and the workforce was larger and wages for workers were higher than they otherwise would be if U.S. firms had to face foreign competition.

But America's corporate and financial elites gradually came to see the economic advantages of expanding world trade (see figure 2.1). U.S. firms that dominated the domestic market in the 1950s and 1960s (steel, automobiles, aircraft, computers, drugs, electronics, agriculture, and so on) began to look abroad to expand their own sales. American corporations became multinational corporations. They began by expanding their sales and distribution staffs worldwide, and then later began to shift manufacturing itself to low-wage, low-cost countries.

Globalization of economic power required reductions in tariffs and trade barriers around the world. America's corporate and financial elites began to lobby Congress for reductions in U.S. tariffs. The result was a rapid decline in average U.S. tariff rates (see figure 2.2, p. 22). In effect, the United States became an open market.

International economic agreements and organizations were arranged in order to facilitate the new global economy. Leadership in global economic policy was provided by the Council on Foreign Relations (CFR) and its multinational arm, the Trilateral Commission (see chapter 3). The Trilateral Commission was created by CFR Board Chairman David Rockefeller in 1972 to bring together a small group of top economic elites from the United States, Western Europe, and Japan.

In addition to initiating annual economic summits of the presidents and prime ministers of the wealthy, industrialized nations, this new global elite put

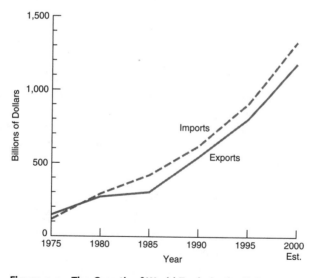

Figure 2.1   The Growth of World Trade in the U.S. Economy

Source: Data from *Statistical Abstract of the United States, 1999.*

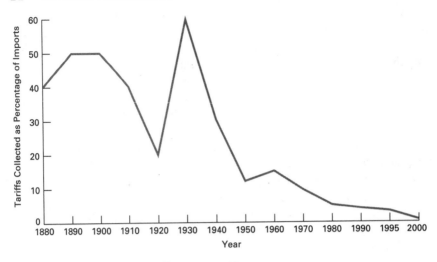

Figure 2.2 Average U.S. Tariff Rates over Time

in place a series of policy decisions designed to advance international trade, including the General Agreement on Tariffs and Trade (GATT), the World Trade Organization (WTO), the World Bank and International Monetary Fund (IMF), and the North American Free Trade Agreement (NAFTA). (See feature: "Deciding on Global Trade Policy," pp. 27–29.)

America's "multinationals"—its largest value exporting industrial corporations—are shown in table 2.5. Some corporations rank higher in exporting than in overall industrial output (compare the entries in table 2.5 with those in table 2.1, p. 18). These include the aircraft manufacturer Boeing; defense-oriented corporations McDonnell Douglas, Lockheed Martin, and United Technologies; computer manufacturers Intel, Compaq Computer, and Digital Equipment; and the giant agricultural exporter Archer Daniels Midland. Yet the largest industrial corporations in America—General Motors and Ford Motor—are also the nation's top exporters.

THE GLOBAL ELITE

The globalization of economic power has created a global elite—the leaders of the *world's* largest banks industrial corporations. The economic power of the global elite challenges the notion of national "sovereignty." This elite can move, or threaten to move, economic resources—industrial plants, sales and inventory, and capital investment—across national boundaries, and thus shape the economic policies of national government. And direct international investments and cross-national ownership of economic resources are rising rapidly. Foreign investment in the United States has risen dramatically since 1980. Foreign firms now invest more in the United States economy than the United States invests abroad (see figure 2.3, p. 24).

Only seventeen of the world's fifty largest industrial corporations are head-

Table 2.5   America's Largest Exporters

Rank	Company Name	Major Export	Value of Exports (in Billions of Dollars)
1.	General Motors	Motor vehicles and parts, locomotives	16.1
2.	Ford Motor	Motor vehicles and parts	11.9
3.	Boeing	Commercial aircraft	11.8
4.	Chrysler	Motor vehicles and parts	9.4
5.	General Electric	Jet engines, turbines, plastics, medical systems, locomotives	8.1
6.	Motorola	Communications equipment, semiconductors	7.4
7.	International Business Machines (IBM)	Computers and related equipment	6.3
8.	Philip Morris	Tobacco, beer, food products	4.9
9.	Archer Daniels Midland	Protein meals, vegetable oils, flour, alcohol, grain	4.7
10.	Hewlett-Packard	Measurement, computation, communications products, and systems	4.7
11.	Intel	Microcomputer components, modules, systems	4.6
12.	Caterpillar	Engines; turbines; construction, mining, and agricultural machinery	4.5
13.	McDonnell Douglas	Aerospace products, missiles, electronic systems	4.2
14.	DuPont	Chemicals, polymers, fibers, specialty products	3.6
15.	United Technologies	Jet engines, helicopters, cooling equipment	3.1
16.	Eastman Kodak	Imaging products	2.6
17.	Lockheed Martin	Aerospace products, missiles, electronic systems	2.1
18.	Compaq Computer	Computers and related equipment	2.0
19.	Raytheon	Electronic systems, engineering and construction projects	1.9
20.	Digital Equipment	Computers, software, related equipment	1.8
21.	AlliedSignal	Aircrafts and automotive parts, chemicals	1.8
22.	Minnesota Mining & Mfg. (3M)	Industrial, electronics, health care, consumer, and imaging products	1.8
23.	Westinghouse Electric	Power systems, office furniture, transport refrigeration	1.6
24.	Dow Chemical	Chemicals, plastics, consumer specialties	1.6
25.	Merck	Health products	1.6

quartered in the United States (see table 2.6, pp. 24–25). General Motors and Ford Motor sit precariously atop the world corporate structure, but Japan, despite a smaller overall economy, has more global sales than the United States. Eighteen of the world's fifty largest corporations are headquartered in Japan. *No* U.S. bank, including America's largest, Citicorp, is among the world's ten largest banks.

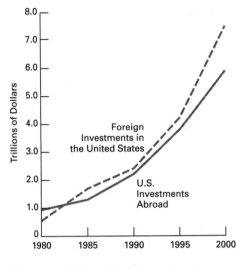

Figure 2.3   International Investment

Source: Data from *Statistical Abstract of the United States 1999*, 793.

Table 2.6   The World's Largest Industrial Corporations

Rank	Company Name	Country
1.	General Motors	United States
2.	Ford Motor	United States
3.	Mitsui	Japan
4.	Mitsubishi	Japan
5.	Exxon	United States
6.	Itochu Shoji	Japan
7.	Marubeni	Japan
8.	Sumitomo	Japan
9.	Toyota Motor	Japan
10.	Wal-Mart	United States
11.	Mobil	United States
12.	General Electric	United States
13.	Nissho Iwai	Japan
14.	Nippon Telegraph and Telephone	Japan
15.	IBM	United States
16.	British Petroleum	United Kingdom
17.	Hitachi	Japan
18.	Philip Morris	United States
19.	Matsushita Electric Industrial	Japan
20.	Royal Dutch Petroleum	Netherlands
21.	Chrysler	United States
22.	Daimler-Benz	Germany

Table 2.6   *(continued)*

Rank	Company Name	Country
23.	Nissan Motor	Japan
24.	Volkswagen	Germany
25.	Unilever	United Kingdom
26.	Shell Transport & Trading	United Kingdom
27.	Siemens	Germany
28.	AT&T	United States
29.	Allianz	Germany
30.	Sony	Japan
31.	Toshiba	Japan
32.	Honda Motor	Japan
33.	Tomen	Japan
34.	Fiat	Italy
35.	Texaco	United States
36.	Unilever	Netherlands
37.	Tokyo Electric Power	Japan
38.	Chevron	United States
39.	DuPont	United States
40.	NEC	Japan
41.	Nestlé	Switzerland
42.	Ell Aquitaine	France
43.	Fujitsu	Germany
44.	VEBA	Germany
45.	Jardine Strategic	Singapore
46.	Hewlett-Packard	United States
47.	Sears, Roebuck	United States
48.	Deutsche Telekom	Germany
49.	Amoco	United States
50.	Proctor & Gamble	United States

INCREASING INEQUALITY IN AMERICA

Overall, the U.S. economy has performed very well in recent years under the policies initiated by the global elite. But the benefits of that performance have been very unevenly distributed. The global economy has produced growth and profit for America's largest corporations (see figure 2.4, p. 26), and it has raised the aggregate income of the nation. But at the same time, it has contributed to a decline in average earnings of American workers and an increase in inequality in America.

The earnings of American workers have declined dramatically with the growth of international trade. In real dollars (controlling for the effects of inflation), average hourly earnings declined from $8.10 in 1970 to $7.40 in 1995, recovering somewhat to $7.75 in 1998 (see figure 2.5, p. 26). The earnings of unskilled and semi-skilled workers have fallen even more dramatically by 25 to 33 percent since 1980.

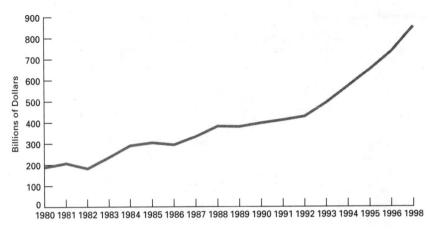

Figure 2.4   Growth in U.S. Corporate Profits

Declining real wages in United States have been obscured by the fact that median family income has been rising. In 1970 median family income was $38,345 (in constant 1997 dollars); by 1997 this figure had risen to $44,568.[4] But family income rose because more family members entered the workforce, not because workers were paid more. Workforce participation among married women rose from 40 percent in 1970 to 62 percent in 1998.[5] In short, American families raised their incomes despite lower hourly wages simply by having more family members go to work.

The global economy offers a huge supply of less skilled labor that is pushing down the wages of American workers. It is difficult to maintain wage levels

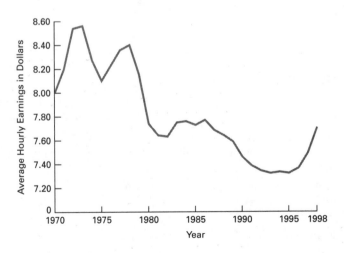

Figure 2.5   Decline in Worker Earnings

FEATURE: DECIDING ON GLOBAL TRADE POLICY

America's elite became "internationalist" in the aftermath of World War II. The earlier "protectionist" stand of America's business and financial leaders was replaced by a global perspective. The American economy in 1945 was by far most powerful in the world. Given their dominant positions in the global economy, key U.S. corporations—especially large exporters such as General Electric, IBM, Caterpillar, DuPont, Philip Morris, R.J. Reynolds, and the defense industries, Boeing, Hewlett-Packard, and Lockheed Martin—began to expand into the global marketplace. To do so meant *lowering* America's historically high tariffs and creating new global organizations in international banking to facilitate world trade.

The elite private policy-planning organizations—the Council on Foreign Relations, the Committee on Economic Development, the Business Council, and later the Business Roundtable—led the way in formulating new international trade policy. Internationalist-minded elites—labeled the "Eastern internationalists"—took control of the Republican Party in 1952, nominating General Dwight D. Eisenhower over the traditional protectionist Robert Taft. The remaining "protectionists" in Congress were soon overwhelmed, and the nation embarked on a series of policy initiatives designed to create a global economy.

Lower Tariffs. Tariffs are taxes on foreign imports. Prior to World War II, U.S. tariffs on all imported goods averaged 30 to 50 percent. This eliminated most foreign competition from U.S. markets. It allowed U.S. firms that were less efficient than foreign producers to survive and prosper in a sheltered market. The pressure to cut wages and downsize workforces was less than it would be if U.S. corporations had to confront foreign competition. But high tariffs invite retaliation by other nations, closing off their markets to U.S. firms. U.S. exporters may be adversely affected by the resulting trade wars. More importantly, the inability of foreign nations to sell products in United States prevented them from acquiring U.S. dollars. Lowering tariffs allowed foreign corporations to sell products in the United States and provided them with U.S. dollars which they could use to purchase the goods of American exporting industries. Today U.S. tariffs average less than 3 percent of the value of all imports. The U.S. dollar has become the principal currency for international trade.

The World Trade Organization. A multinational General Agreement on Tariffs and Trade organization was created following World War II for the purpose of encouraging international trade. Over the years GATT has been dominated by banking, business, and commercial interests in Western nations seeking multilateral tariff reductions and the relaxation of quotas. In 1993 the GATT "Uruguay Round" eliminated quotas on textile products; established more uniform standards for proof of dumping; set rules for the protection of intellectual property rights (patents and copyrights on books, movies, videos, and so on); reduced tariffs on wood, paper, and some other raw materials; and scheduled a gradual reduction of government subsidies for agricultural products.

The World Trade Organization was created in 1993. Today WTO includes 130 nations that agree to a governing set of global trade rules. (China and Russia have applied to join.) The WTO is given power to adjudicate trade disputes among countries and monitor and enforce trade agreements.

The International Monetary Fund and the World Bank. The IMF's purpose is to facilitate international trade, allowing nations to borrow to stabilize their balance of trade payments. When economically weak nations, however, incur chronic balance of trade deficits and perhaps face deferral or default on international debts, the IMF may condition its loans on changes in a nation's economic policies. It may require a reduction in a nation's government deficits by reduced public spending and/or higher taxes; or it may require a devaluation of its currency, making its exports cheaper and imports more expensive. It may also require the adoption of noninflationary monetary policies. Currently, the IMF as well as the World Bank are actively involved in assisting Russia and other states of the former Soviet Union convert to free market economies.

The World Bank makes long-term loans, mostly to developing nations, to assist in economic development. It works closely with the IMF in investigating the economic conditions of nations applying for loans and generally imposes IMF requirements on these nations as conditions for loans.

NAFTA. In 1993 the United States, Canada, and Mexico signed the North American Free Trade Agreement. Objections by labor unions in the United States (and independent presidential candidate Ross Perot) were drowned out in a torrent of support by the American corporate community, Democrats and Republicans in Congress, President Bill Clinton, and former President George Bush. NAFTA envisions the removal of tariffs on virtually all products by all three nations over a period of ten to fifteen years. It also allows banking, insurance, and other financial services to cross these borders.

Elite Consensus. Both Democratic and Republican presidential administrations over the past half-century have supported expanded world trade. The

U.S. market is the largest in the world and the most open to foreign-made goods. U.S. policy has been to maintain an open market while encouraging other nations to do the same. Opposition to these policies from American workers and labor unions have been ignored. Indeed, the United States continues to lead international efforts to further liberalize world trade, encourage the flow of investment capital around the world, and eliminate foreign market barriers to American exports. Indeed, in 2000 elite pressure overcame the opposition of unions, environmentalists, and human rights organizations and inspired Congress to grant "permanent normal trading" status to China.

in United States, especially in labor-intensive industries, in the face of labor competition from Mexico, China, Philippines, Indonesia, and other Third World countries. American corporations may initially respond by increasing their investment in capital and technology, making American workers more productive and better able to maintain their high wages. But over time, developing nations are acquiring more capital and technology themselves. Moreover, U.S. corporations are moving their manufacturing plants to low-wage countries, for example to northern Mexico where the transportation costs of moving finished products back into the U.S. market are minimal.

Indeed, American corporations have thrived on international trade expansion, raising the incomes of their executives as well as their most highly skilled workers. But the combined effects of *higher* wages for executives and highly skilled workers and *lower* wages for less skilled workers worsens inequality in the nation.

The prosperous 1990s brought very dramatic differences in income growth for workers versus corporations, their chief executives, and stock market investors. Average workers wages (not adjusted for inflation) rose 27 percent. But corporate profits rose 105 percent, chief executive salaries rose 163 percent, and the S&P stock average rose 218 percent![6] It may be true that rising waters lift all boats, but yachts appear to be floating higher than dinghies.

Both income and wealth are less evenly distributed among the American people today than in 1970. The poorest one-fifth of American families received 5.4 percent of all family *income* in 1970, but by 1998 their share of all family income had declined to 4.2 percent. In contrast, the richest one-fifth of American families increased their share of total family income from 40.9 percent to 46.9 percent (see figure 2.6, p. 30).

The economic boom of the 1990s temporarily halted the growth of inequality. The tight labor market created by economic growth provided more jobs, more hours of work, and better hourly wages for people at the low end of the

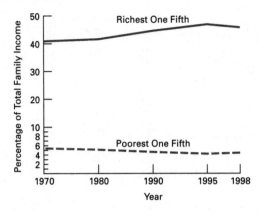

Figure 2.6   Income Inequality in America

workforce. And the poor in America increased their standard of living. It is some-times argued that inequality may be justified if the rich grow richer and the poor are no worse off. Low-income families, however, have maintained living standards only by having fewer children, putting more members to work for longer hours, and running up debt. The *lowest* income earners—the lowest one-fifth of all income earners—actually lost income since 1980 (see figure 2.7). Most of the gains were concentrated among the highest income earners.

Inequality of *wealth* in the United States is even greater than inequality of income. Wealth is the net value of a family's assets—bank accounts, stocks, bonds, mutual funds, houses, cars, and so on—minus outstanding debt, such as credit card balances, mortgages, and other unpaid loans. The top 1 percent of families in United States owns almost 40 percent of all family wealth in the nation.[7]

The rise in wealth inequality since 1970 is striking. The top 1 percent of wealth holders increased their share of total wealth from roughly 20 percent to 40 percent over the past thirty years. It is estimated that virtually all of the increase in the nation's wealth in the past thirty years has accrued to only the top 20 percent of wealth holders.[8]

Perhaps not all of these changes can be attributed to the growth of interna-tional trade and policy decisions by America's elite that encouraged economic globalization. But Harvard economist Richard B. Freeman summarizes the distressing trends in the American economic and social structure:

> An economic disaster has befallen low-skilled Americans, especially young men. Researchers using several data sources—including household survey data from the Current Population Survey, other household surveys, and establishment surveys—have documented that wage inequality and skill differentials in earnings and employment increased sharply in the United

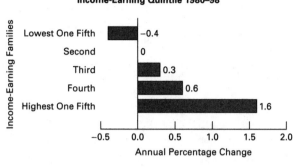

**Average Annual Change in Family by
Income-Earning Quintile 1980–98**

Figure 2.7   Unequal Family Income Growth

Source: U.S. News & World Report, 24 May 1999.

States from the mid-1970s through the 1980s and into the 1990s. The drop in the relative position of the less skilled shows up in a number of ways: greater earnings differentials between those with more and less education; greater earnings differentials between older and younger workers; greater differentials between high-skilled and low-skilled occupations; in a wider earnings distribution overall and within demographic and skill groups; and in less time worked by low-skill and low-paid workers.[9]

INEQUALITY AS A "NONDECISION"

Inequality has traditionally been a "nondecision" in American politics. Indeed, the United States may be unique among nations in the absence of political conflict over economic inequality. It certainly was the intention of the Founders to suppress this most "factious" of issues—"an equal division of property."[10] The notion of equality of results, or absolute equality, was denounced as "leveling" by Thomas Jefferson, and generally has been denounced by the nation's elite then and now:

> To take from one, because it is thought his own industry and that of his fathers has acquired too much, in order to spare to others who have not exercised equal industry and skill, is to violate arbitrarily . . . the guarantee to everyone the free exercise of his industry and the fruits acquired by it.[11]

The American "ethos" emphasizes *equality of opportunity*—the elimination of artificial barriers to success in life. Americans are virtually unanimous in their belief that "Everyone should have equal opportunity to get ahead."[12] They believe that talent and ability and industry should be rewarded with higher income. They do not resent the fact that individuals who have spent time and energy acquiring particular skills make more money than those whose jobs require fewer skills and less training. Neither do they resent the fact that people who risk time and money to build a business, bring new products to market, and create jobs for others, make more money than their employees. Indeed, few Americans object when someone wins a million-dollar lottery, as long as everyone had an equal chance to enter and win.[13]

But absolute equality, or *equality of results,* holds little appeal for Americans generally. Government efforts to reduce income inequality, supported by majorities in most other Western democracies, receive little support from Americans. In cross-national surveys asking the question "Is it the government's responsibility to reduce income differences among people?" about 60 percent of Western Europeans say "Yes," while only 28 percent of Americans do so.[14] Support among Americans for the unlimited accumulation of wealth extends to all income levels, although not surprisingly it appears significantly more popular among the rich (see table 2.7).

America's national elite is aware, of course, of these "latent" issues—declining real wages and worsening inequality. Their response is to stress the need for American workers to improve their productivity through better education and increased training. A surprisingly candid Economic Report of the President recommends the following:

> Ultimately, the only lasting solution to the increase in wage inequality that results from increased trade is the same as that for wage inequality arising from any other source: better education and increased training to allow

Table 2.7   Mass Attitudes toward the Accumulation of Wealth

"People should be allowed to accumulate as much wealth as they can even if some make millions while others live in poverty."

	Strongly Agree or Agree	Neither Agree nor Disagree	Strongly Disagree or Disagree
Total	56%	11%	30%
Income level			
Under $15,000	51%	12%	33%
$15,000 to $19,999	59	7	33
$20,000 to $29,999	54	11	34
$30,000 to $49,999	60	11	27
$50,000 to $74,999	60	10	27
$75,000 and up	65	12	22

Source: Everett Carll Ladd and Karlyn H. Bowman, *Attitudes toward Economic Inequality* (Washington, D.C.: American Enterprise Institute Press, 1998).

low-income workers to take advantage of the technological changes that raise productivity.[15]

The recommendation implies that the fault lies with the ignorance and incompetence of American workers, not with any trade policies decided on by elites.

THE MAKING OF A NONDECISION

The nation's elite is fully aware of the importance of keeping the issue of income distribution "latent." The prescription for doing so is threefold: (1) maintain support for a national "ethos" that separates economic outcomes from political activity; (2) maintain aggregate growth of the economy and the resulting trickle-down increases in the material well-being of the masses; (3) maintain opportunity (or at least the belief in opportunity) for upward social mobility.

Maintain the National Ethos

Americans generally distinguish between the *private economic* sphere of life and the *public political* sphere. In the private economic sphere, they recognize the principal of "earned deserts"—individuals are entitled to what they achieve through hard work, skill, talent, risk, and even good luck. Inequality that results from earned deserts are acceptable. Self-interested behavior in the private market-place is viewed as appropriate, even beneficial. Very few Americans want to place a "ceiling" on income or wealth.

In the public political sphere, however, Americans value absolute equality—one person, one vote. They condemn disparities of political power among citizens, including disparities arising from differences in wealth. Self-interested behavior in politics and public affairs are viewed as corrupt.

The key to maintaining these contrasting views about equality is to continue to separate the economic and political spheres of life—to continue to view economic activities as largely private and separate from politics.

Maintain Aggregate Economic Growth

Nothing inspires support for the prevailing political system more than prosperity. Rising material standards of living for the masses keep the issue of inequality "latent." A booming stock market, a federal budget in the black, low inflation, and most of all, increasing material well-being, obscure inequality.

Despite lagging real hourly wages, Americans actually enjoy a higher standard living than they did twenty or even ten years ago. The data on *consumption* in contrast to *income* clearly indicates that even the poor are better off today than they were only a few years ago. That is to say, they are more likely to own automobiles, color television sets, washing machines, and other luxu-

FEATURE: DECIDING TO GRANT PREFERENTIAL TAX TREATMENT TO INVESTORS

Investors' profits from capital transactions—buying and selling of stocks, bonds, real estate, and so forth—are given preferential treatment in federal tax laws over workers who earn their income in wages and salaries. Why should "unearned income"—capital gains—be given preferential treatment over "earned income"—wages and salaries?

For decades capital gains enjoyed a huge tax preference in federal income tax laws. Only one-half of an investor's capital gains were counted as taxable income, in effect granting a 50 percent tax break. But in the Tax Reform Act of 1986, Congress and President Ronald Reagan succeeded in eliminating preferential treatment for capital gains. In exchange for a lower top tax rate (28 percent), various tax loopholes were closed, including the tax break for capital gains. All types of income, earned and unearned, were to be taxed at the same rates. But was not long before powerful interests, notably Wall Street investment firms, the real estate industry, and wealthy investors, succeeded in reintroducing preferential treatment for capital gains.

Income from capital gains is concentrated among the wealthiest portion of the nation's population. Taxpayers with incomes of $100,000 or more (the top 5 percent of all households) reap 76 percent of these gains. Taxpayers with incomes of $200,000 or more (the top 1 percent of all households) received 62 percent of all capital gains (see figure 2A).

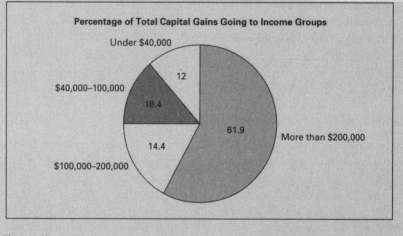

Percentage of Total Capital Gains Going to Income Groups

Under $40,000 — 12
$40,000–100,000 — 18.4
$100,000–200,000 — 14.4
More than $200,000 — 61.9

Figure 2A

Source: Congressional Budget Office. Data reported in *Congressional Quarterly Weekly Report*, 7 June 1997, 1300.

Many Congress members are reluctant to go on record as voting in favor of a tax break that clearly favors the rich. Yet, as observed in chapter 4, the bulk of political campaign contributions come from the wealthiest portions of the population. Republicans in Congress have been more open in their support for preferential (lower) tax rates on capital gains. Democrats have been more circumspect in their approach to the issue, preferring to sneak preferential treatment into the tax laws without many Americans knowing about it.

In 1991, with Democrats in control of Congress and Republican George Bush in the White House, the top income tax rate was raised from 28 to 31 percent. (Bush would later suffer at the polls for violating his solemn pledge "Read my lips! No new taxes!") But Bush and congressional Democrats quietly made the new top rate applicable only to "earned" income, that is, to income from wages and salaries. The top rate on capital gains remained at 28 percent. Hardly anyone noticed the reintroduction of this preferential treatment.

In 1993 Democrat Bill Clinton and a Democratic-controlled Congress raised the top income tax rate to 39.6 percent. Again they quietly made the new rate applicable only to "earned" income, leaving the capital gains tax rate at 28 percent. This, of course, widened the preference given to capital gains. (It should also be noted that capital gains income is not taxed until the asset—stocks, bonds, real estate, etc.—is sold; investors may at their option defer sale and hence payment of the tax as long as they wish. In contrast, taxes on wages and salaries must be paid when they are earned.) Few Americans took notice of how a major announced goal of tax reform—treating all types of income equally—became undone.

When Republicans took control of Congress following the 1994 midterm congressional election, they were unrestrained in their support for even further reductions in capital gains taxation. A reduction was assured when Democratic President Bill Clinton announced his support for a reduction in taxes on capital gains. While giving rhetorical support to tax reductions generally, Republicans managed only to cut capital gains taxes. The top rate was lowered to 20 percent in 1997. This capital gains tax reduction was sandwiched into a larger "deficit reduction" budget act that was eagerly signed by President Clinton. (Few Americans questioned the contradictory phraseology—that "deficit reduction" included a further lowering of taxes on capital gains.) Today, the top income tax rate on workers' wages and salaries (39.6%) is nearly twice as high as the top rate on investors' capital gains (20%) (see figure 2B, p. 36).

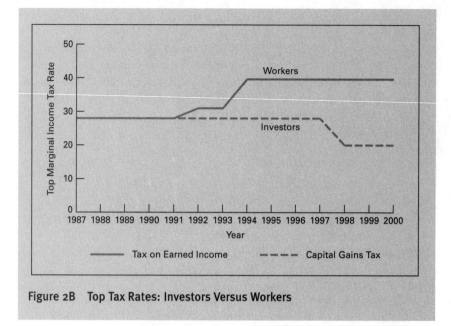

Figure 2B Top Tax Rates: Investors Versus Workers

ries (see table 2.8). Moreover, their material goods are better today than they used to be. Automobiles have air conditioning, stereos, antilock brakes, air bags, antipollution devices, and so on. Homes have air conditioning, two-car garages, extra bathrooms, and other amenities. Health care now includes CAT scans, heart bypass surgery, organ transplants, and other advanced treatments and procedures not available twenty years ago; and Americans have come to consider high-quality health care a right. Life expectancy continues to increase, infant mortality rates are decreasing, and death rates from most diseases are declining.

Table 2.8 Even the Poor Have More (in percentages)

	Poor Households 1984	Poor Households 1994	All Households 1971
Households with:			
Washing machine	58.2	71.7	71.3
Microwave	12.5	60.0	‹1.0
Color television	70.3	92.5	43.3
Dishwasher	13.6	19.6	18.8
One or more cars	64.1	71.8	79.5

Source: W. Michael Cox and Richard Alm, *Myths of the Rich and Poor* (New York: Basic Books, 1998).

Elites from all sectors of society are interested and active in maintaining economic growth. Indeed, economic growth is the single most widely shared value in elite circles. Presidents, members of Congress, corporate chieftains, media moguls, and foundation and civic group leaders all understand the importance of maintaining the material well-being of the masses. "Saving" Social Security, Medicare, and Medicaid is more than Washington rhetoric. It is widely understood among elites that the continuation of these programs is essential to maintain political stability.

Maintain Social Mobility

America has always described itself as the land of opportunity. And, indeed, social mobility in the United States has historically distinguished our nation from the more class-conscious and class-bounded nations of Western Europe.

Steep inequalities of wealth and income are tolerated politically when people believe that they have a reasonable expectation of moving up over time, or at least of seeing their children do so. And certainly the belief in social mobility in America remains high (see table 2.9).

Is this belief justified? Historically, the answer has been "yes." That is to say, there has been considerable evidence of upward (as well as downward) social mobility among income groupings. About one-third of the families in the poorest one-fifth of income earners will move upward to a higher income group within a decade. About one-third of families in the richest one-fifth will fall out of this top category. Intergenerational income mobility is even greater (see figure 2.8, p. 38).

Table 2.9   Americans' Belief in Social Mobility

Question: Some people say there's not much opportunity in America today—that the average person doesn't have much chance to really get ahead. Others say there's plenty of opportunity and anyone who works hard can go as far as they want. How do you feel about this?

Plenty of opportunity	83%
Not much opportunity	17%

Question: Is there more opportunity in America today for the average person to really get ahead than there used to be, less opportunity for the average person to really get ahead, or is the amount of opportunity about the same?

More opportunity	43%
About the same	36%
Less opportunity	20%

Source: Survey by the Gallup Organization, 23 April–31 May 1998, as reported in *The Public Perspective*, April/May 1999.

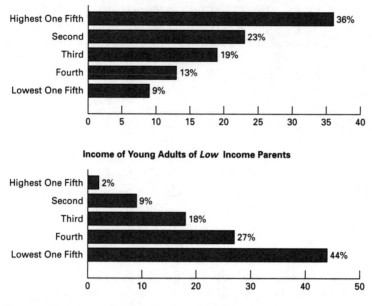

Income of Young Adults of *High* Income Parents

Figure 2.8   Intergenerational Income Mobility

Source: Panel Study of Income Dynamics, University of Michigan Survey Research Center.

Note: The figure shows the percentage of young adults whose parents' income was in the highest and lowest quintiles, who ended up in various income quintiles themselves. Thus, for example, only 36 percent of the children of highest income parents ended up in the highest income quintile themselves. A few (9 percent) ended up in the lowest quintile. Among offspring of lowest-income quintile families, 44 percent ended up in the lowest quintile themselves, but more than half moved up to higher income quintiles, including a few (2 percent) who rose to the highest quintile.

This mobility may have slowed, however, in recent years. One's chances of escaping the bottom may be diminishing; income group boundaries may be strengthening. If so, and if the perception of class mobility fades, the "latent" issue of income inequality might become manifest.

CHAPTER 3

The Policy Formulation Process

Governments don't have time to think about the broader longer-range issues. It seemed to make sense to persuade a group of private, qualified citizens to get together to identify the key issues affecting the world and possible solutions.

—DAVID ROCKEFELLER

POLICY FORMULATION OCCURS from the top down—when institutional leaders, primarily in business, finance, and the media, begin to complain about societal developments they perceive as threatening to their own values or interests. For example, inasmuch as economic growth is the most pervasive elite value, potential limits on growth are rather quickly identified, discussed, and placed on the nation's policymaking agenda. A particular condition in society that does not directly affect elite interests, however, is unlikely to be identified as a "problem" or to be given much discussion in the boardrooms of corporations, banks, or media conglomerates. This is *not* to say, however, that enlightened elites do not occasionally anticipate mass discontent that might arise from problems which more directly affect masses than elites.

Agenda setting and policy formulation begin well before any actions by government or government officials. According to sociologist G. William Domhoff,

> The policy-formation process begins informally in corporate boardrooms, social clubs, and discussion groups, where problems are identified as "issues" to be solved by new policies. It ends in government, where policies are enacted and implemented. In between, however, there is a complex network of people and institutions that play an important role in sharpening the issues and weighing the alternatives.[1]

TOP-DOWN POLICY FORMULATION

The agenda-setting and policy formulation process flows downward from elites to government through a network of foundations, "think tanks," policy planning organizations, and the media. Figure 3.1 (p. 40) portrays this top-down policy formulation process.

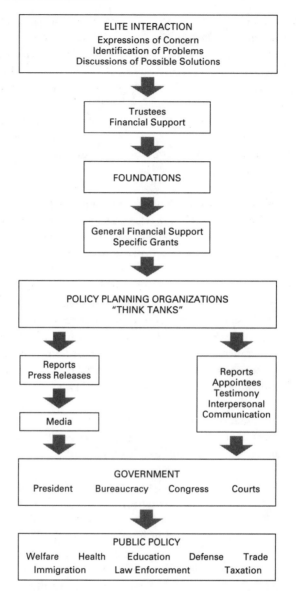

ELITE INTERACTION
Expressions of Concern
Identification of Problems
Discussions of Possible Solutions

Trustees
Financial Support

FOUNDATIONS

General Financial Support
Specific Grants

POLICY PLANNING ORGANIZATIONS
"THINK TANKS"

Reports
Press Releases

Reports
Appointees
Testimony
Interpersonal
Communication

Media

GOVERNMENT
President   Bureaucracy   Congress   Courts

PUBLIC POLICY
Welfare   Health   Education   Defense   Trade
Immigration   Law Enforcement   Taxation

Figure 3.1   The Top-Down Policy Formulation Process

Corporate and personal wealth are channeled into foundations. Foundations are tax-free institutions that provide grants of money to nonprofit organizations, ranging from policy planning "think tanks" to medical research centers, colleges and universities, and art museums. Federal tax laws encourage corporations and wealthy individuals to protect their assets by creating foundations to accumulate and distribute wealth. Corporate directors and wealthy individuals who establish foundations and make contributions to them usually name themselves and their friends as directors or trustees. Thus, the trustees of the nation's major foundations are elites themselves—corporate and bank presidents and directors, media moguls, and top wealth holders. Large foundations have executive directors and staff to sift through the tens of thousands of requests for financial support that flow into the foundations every year. But it is the foundation trustees that identify priorities, determine the direction of financial flows, and oversee spending of foundation funds.

The foundations largely determine the agenda of the nation's policy planning organizations. Foundations provide the money to identify social problems, determine national priorities, and investigate new policy directions. Of course, some suggestions flow upward when think tank personnel submit proposals for the funding of new policy research. But research proposals originating from think tanks, as well as from universities, that do not fit the previously defined "emphasis" of a foundation are usually lost in the shuffle of papers. Intellectuals working in think tanks and universities primarily *respond* to the policy directions set by the foundations.

Policy planning organizations, or "think tanks," are the central coordinating mechanisms in the top down policy formulation process. Specific policy recommendations and supporting research are developed in the nation's leading think tanks. It is here that previously identified "problems" are defined in detail and specific "solutions" developed. The reports and recommendations developed in the think tanks and published in their books, journals, and magazines provide both blueprints and previews of what soon will become policy discussions in the news media and in Washington.

The policy planning organizations not only identify the nation's problems and devise solutions to them, they also endeavor to develop a consensus among national elites, the mass media, interest groups, government officials, and political leaders. Indeed, the major think tanks devote considerable energy and resources to the dissemination and promotion of their policy recommendations. They frequently invite media representatives, White House officials, and key members of Congress to meet with the authors of policy recommendations. They offer testimony at congressional committee hearings, submit commentary regarding proposed regulations to executive agencies, mobilize interest groups on behalf their recommendations, and, perhaps most importantly, talk to their friends in government.

The policy recommendations of the think tanks are distributed to the mass media, usually in the form of press releases, as well as directly to the White House, executive agencies, and Congress. The media play an important independent role in the policymaking process (see chapter 6). Their decisions about what is "news" sets the agenda for public discussion. The media decide what the American people as well as their government officials will talk about.

Government officials, the "proximate policymakers," merely legitimize and implement policies formulated by others. It is true that in the course of legitimizing and implementing policy, the proximate policymakers may add clauses, conditions, amendments, and interpretations that affect policy itself. But these additions are usually no more than incremental changes. They may not be unimportant, especially to those directly affected by the policies, but these details are decided within the context of goals and directions of public policy that have already been determined.

THE FOUNDATIONS

The power of the nation's leading foundations derives from their financial support of the policy formulation process. There are more than 10,000 foundations in the United States with assets of at least $2 million.[2] Collectively these foundations control more than $300 billion in assets and distribute nearly $15 billion in grants each year. But, as in other sectors of society, foundation assets are concentrated in a small number of large foundations. Indeed, the thirty-eight foundations (with $1 billion or more in assets) listed in table 3.1 control about 50 percent of all foundation assets in the nation.

Historically, most of the large foundations were established by America's wealthiest families—Ford, Rockefeller, Carnegie, Mellon, Pew, Duke, Lilly, Kellogg, Getty, Packard, and so on. Over the years, however, some foundations—notably Ford, Rockefeller, and Carnegie—became independent of their original family ties. This independence occurs when original family investments prosper and the foundations generate their own income. Family members are gradually eased off of the governing boards of trustees. Thus, for example, no Ford family members currently are trustees of the Ford Foundation and no Rockefellers are trustees of the Rockefeller Foundation.

The financial support for national policy formulation comes largely from a very few of these large foundations. (Some large foundations spend their funds on museums, opera houses, historic preservations, theater, and the arts; these types of foundations have little policy impact. The William H. Gates Foundation, for example, endowed with $20 billion in 2000 by America's richest entrepreneur, buys computers for schools and supports Boys and Girls Clubs of America. It is currently the nation's wealthiest foundation.) But a few top foundations—for example, Ford, Rockefeller, Carnegie—involve themselves in a broad range of policy issues. Some other large foundations concentrate their attention on special policy fields; for example, Robert Wood Johnson specializes in health care policy.

Historically, the Ford, Rockefeller, and Carnegie foundations led the way in providing financial support for the nation's policy formulation process (see table 3.2, p. 47). Today the Ford Foundation is the nation's largest and most influen-

Table 3.1   The Billion-Dollar Foundations

Rank	Name (state)	Assets
1.	Lilly Endowment Inc. (Ind.)	$11,500,000,000
2.	The Ford Foundation (N.Y.)	9,597,907,967
3.	The David and Lucile Packard Foundation (Calif.)	8,991,300,000
4.	W.K. Kellogg Foundation (Mich.)	7,588,408,314
5.	J. Paul Getty Trust (Calif.)	7,389,565,432
6.	The Robert Wood Johnson Foundation (N.J.)	6,734,918,302
7.	The Pew Charitable Trusts (Pa.)	4,522,480,597
8.	John D. and Catherine T. MacArthur Foundation (Ill.)	4,030,139,783
9.	Robert W. Woodruff Foundation, Inc. (Ga.)	3,680,536,964
10.	The Rockefeller Foundation (N.Y.)	3,094,733,452
11.	The Andrew W. Mellon Foundation (N.Y.)	3,080,437,000
12.	The Annenberg Foundation (Pa.)	2,584,405,699
13.	The Starr Foundation (N.Y.)	2,541,595,582
14.	The Kresge Foundation (Mich.)	2,102,976,862
15.	The Duke Endowment (N.C.)	1,980,446,331
16.	Charles Stewart Mott Foundation (Mich.)	1,963,825,032
17.	The Harry and Jeanette Weinberg Foundation, Inc. (Md.)	1,845,127,300
18.	The William and Flora Hewlett Foundation (Calif.)	1,766,610,354
19.	The California Endowment (Calif.)	1,759,533,900
20.	The McKnight Foundation (Minn.)	1,709,867,516
21.	Ewing Marion Kauffman Foundation (Mo.)	1,649,994,000
22.	The New York Community Trust (N.Y.)	1,588,174,769
23.	Richard King Mellon Foundation (Pa.)	1,531,329,362
24.	Robert R. McCormick Tribune Foundation (Ill.)	1,467,807,068
25.	Carnegie Corporation of New York (N.Y.)	1,441,675,860
26.	W. M. Keck Foundation (Calif.)	1,437,083,000
27.	Houston Endowment, Inc. (Tex.)	1,331,565,238
28.	The Annie E. Casey Foundation (Md.)	1,316,355,130
29.	Doris Duke Charitable Foundation (N.Y.)	1,306,684,800
30.	The Cleveland Foundation (Ohio)	1,269,684,396
31.	The Brown Foundation, Inc. (Tex.)	1,254,789,195
32.	Joseph B. Whitehead Foundation (Ga.)	1,208,954,802
33.	Donald W. Reynolds Foundation (Okla.)	1,194,912,087
34.	John S. and James L. Knight Foundation (Fla.)	1,189,784,367
35.	Alfred P. Sloan Foundation (N.Y.)	1,101,586,214
36.	The California Wellness Foundation (Calif.)	1,075,415,344
37.	The James Irvine Foundation (Calif.)	1,051,258,644
38.	The William Penn Foundation (Pa.)	1,005,604,178

Source: The Foundation Directory 1999.

FEATURE: THE FORD FOUNDATION, FUNDING THE LIBERAL AGENDA

The Ford family launched the Ford Foundation in 1936 as a local Detroit philanthropic organization. But in the 1950s Henry Ford II expanded the foundation into a national policy formulation funding source. He used Ford funds to advance urban renewal and community development movements throughout the country. Detroit's Renaissance Center was only one of many urban projects undertaken by Ford. At the same time, the Mellon family was undertaking the redevelopment of Pittsburgh. In the Housing Act of 1950, the federal government established a grant-in-aid program for urban renewal, and in 1965 the U.S. Department of Housing and Urban Development was created.

In 1951 Henry Ford II asked the president of the University of Chicago, Robert Hutchins, to take over the foundation and make it into a national force in public affairs. The foundation soon undertook to support moderate civil rights organizations, including the Urban League, with Henry Ford's approval. But later Ford dismissed Hutchins for funding some projects that "the Chairman" did not like. Ford turned to McGeorge Bundy to be its president in the late 1960s. (Bundy had been Presidents Kennedy and Johnson's national security adviser and the central figure in America's initial involvement in the Vietnam War.)

But Bundy proceeded to turn the foundation into the single largest source of money for liberal causes throughout the nation. He focused the foundation on the problems of poor and minority populations. Many of the projects funded by Ford in the 1960s were incorporated into President Lyndon B. Johnson's "War on Poverty." Bundy also sold off the foundation's stock in the Ford Motor Company. Bundy and Henry Ford II increasingly clashed over the liberal directions of the foundation. Finally, in 1976, Ford resigned as a trustee of the Ford Foundation. In his resignation letter, he pointedly advised the foundation not to undertake projects that might undermine the capitalist system: "The Foundation is a creature of capitalism. . . . I'm just suggesting to the trustees and the staff that the system that makes the foundation possible very probably is worth preserving."[a]

For many years, the Ford Foundation was the single largest source of revenue for the Brookings Institution (see discussion later in this chapter). A Ford Foundation staff member, Kermit Gordon, served a long term as president of Brookings. Later Ford money would be used to establish the Institute of Policy Studies, Washington's far-left "think tank" (sometimes referred to as the "pink tank").

Since the 1970s the Ford Foundation has been the largest single source of money behind the environmental movement in the nation. The foundation has given large sums of money to the Audubon Society, the Nature Conservancy, and the National Resources Defense Council. These organizations in turn played a major role in creating and then later sustaining political support for the U.S. Environmental Protection Agency (EPA).

Moreover, the Ford Foundation has funded a large number of university and "think tank" studies on pesticides and industrial waste. Finally, it has been a major sponsor of educational programs on environmental protection in public schools. In recent years, the foundation has undertaken to advance a wide variety of policy initiatives to "reduce poverty and injustice," advance "international human rights," promote "peace and social justice," inspire "civic participation," and defend women's "reproductive rights." Heavyweights on the current board of trustees include the presidents of Lucent Technologies, Xerox, and Reuters News and the prominent Washington lawyer Vernon Jordan.

a. Quoted in *Newsweek*, 24 January 1977.

tial source of funds for policy formulation. It is largely responsible for the policy successes of the environmental protection movement, the worldwide movement for human rights, and the abortion rights movement (see feature: The Ford Foundation, Funding the Liberal Agenda).

For many years the Rockefeller Foundation reflected the policy interests of David Rockefeller, chairman of the Chase Manhattan Bank and grandson of the founding tycoon of America's oil industry, John D. Rockefeller. Various Rockefeller investment holding companies, together with Chase Manhattan, held controlling blocks of stock in many other large corporations, including Exxon, Eastern Airlines, Boeing, and Mobil Oil. But the core of the Rockefeller holdings remained in the oil industry, and these holdings required constant attention to foreign sources of supply. In addition, Chase Manhattan became deeply involved in overseas banking and investment activities earlier than most other U.S. banks.

David Rockefeller's interest in foreign affairs led to the foundation's support of the Council on Foreign Relations (CFR). Rockefeller himself assumed the chairmanship of CFR, a post that he did not relinquish until 1985. The CFR in turn became the principal policy planning organization for America's foreign affairs (see discussion later in chapter). Rockefeller also supplied many of the top foreign affairs personnel for the nation, including Secretaries of State John Foster Dulles, Dean Rusk, and Henry Kissinger. Of course, Rockefeller exercised his power with great *modesty:*

> I feel uncomfortable when you ask how I exert power. We accomplish things through cooperative action, which is quite different than exerting power in some mysterious and presumably evil way. I have no power in the sense that I can call anybody in the government and tell them what to do. Because of my position, I'm more apt to get through on the telephone than somebody else, but what happens to what I suggest depends on whether they feel this makes sense in terms of what they are already doing.[3]

The Carnegie Corporation descended from the philanthropic interests of its legendary founder Andrew Carnegie. Carnegie was the founding tycoon of America's steel industry at the end of the nineteenth century. In 1911 he founded the corporation to distribute money to build libraries in virtually every major city in the nation "for the advancement and diffusion of knowledge and understanding among the people of the United States." Today the Carnegie Corporation is best known for its programs in "international peace and security"—nonproliferation of weapons of mass destruction, support for capitalist economic development in Russia, and efforts to reduce terrorism and ethnic strife. In these efforts Carnegie parallels the work of the Rockefeller Foundation and the CFR. Perhaps Carnegie's most controversial policy initiative is political campaign finance reform: "A fundamental source of discontent in the U.S. electorate is abuse of the system of political campaign finance."[4]

The conservative movement in America was late in recognizing the nature of the top-down policy formulation process. Indeed, for many years prominent conservatives bemoaned the fact that they had no institutions comparable to the Ford Foundation or the Brookings Institution. Conservatives complained that the unchallenged preeminence of liberal policy formulation institutions were responsible for the direction of the nation's domestic policies in the 1960s, notably President Lyndon B. Johnson's "Great Society" with its "War on Poverty," Medicare, and Medicaid, and later the creation and empowerment of the Environmental Protection Agency. It was not until the early 1980s that wealthy conservative tycoons—Paul T. Mellon, Richard Scaife, Adolph Coors, Jack Eckerd, John M. Olin, Lewis I. Lehrman—began to channel money through their own foundations to a network of relatively new think tanks.

Perhaps because of their late start in policy formulation, the conservative policy foundations in America have yet to accumulate the wealth and influence of the older established liberal institutions. The leading conservative policy formulation foundations—the Lynde and Harry Bradley Foundation, the Smith Richardson Foundation, and the John M. Olin Foundation—all have less than $1 billion in total assets (see table 3.2).

Table 3.2 Funding the Policy Formulation Process

Foundation	Politics	Policy Interests
Ford Foundation $10 billion	Liberal	"Reduce poverty and injustice"; environmental protection; civic participation by the poor; international human rights; reproductive (abortion) rights.
Rockefeller Foundation $3 billion	Moderate	Global economic development; population control; world energy policy; institutional development in Africa.
Carnegie Corporation $1.5 billion	Moderate	Child care; education; race/intergroup relations; campaign finance reform.
Robert Wood Johnson Foundation $7 billion	Moderate	National health insurance for children; "Partnership for a Drug Free America"; antitobacco legislation; health care for the aged.
MacArthur Foundation $4 billion	Moderate	Global environment protection; "global warming"; global security and arms reduction.
Lilly Endowment $12 billion	Moderate	Religion, education, and community development; "volunteerism" research; support for the economically disadvantaged.
Lynde and Harry Bradley Foundation $0.6 billion	Conservative	Decentralize institutions of government; "Reinvigorate and reempower" families, churches, neighborhoods.
Smith Richardson Foundation $0.5 billion	Conservative	Tax limits; school choice; union dues in politics.
John M. Olin Foundation $0.5 billion	Conservative	Regulatory reform; strengthen "moral and culture principles underlying the Constitution"; tax reduction.
Scaife Foundations	Conservative	Public policy research; issues relating to the family; law enforcement.

THE THINK TANKS

Policy planning organizations, or "think tanks," are at the center of the policy formulation process. They turn money into policy options.

Certain policy planning organizations—notably the Brookings Institution, the American Enterprise Institute, and the Heritage Foundation—are influential in a wide variety of policy areas. The Council on Foreign Relations and its multinational arm, the Trilateral Commission, have become *global* think tanks, promoting policy planning among elites from all of the developed democracies. (We shall describe them in the next section.) Other policy planning organizations may specialize in certain policy areas, for example, the Urban Institute in the problems of the inner city, Resources for the Future in environmental issues, and the Population Council in world population control. We have selected what we believe to be the most influential broad-based policy planning organizations to illustrate their importance in policy formulation.

The Brookings Institution

The Brookings Institution has long dominated American domestic policy planning. The *New York Times* columnist and Harvard historian writing team, Leonard and Mark Silk, describe Brookings as the central locus of the Washington "policy network" where it does "its communicating: over lunch, whether informally in the Brookings cafeteria or at the regular Friday lunch around a great oval table at which the staff and their guests keen over the events of the week like the chorus of an ancient Greek tragedy; through consulting, paid or unpaid, for government or business at conferences, in the advanced studies program; and, over time, by means of the revolving door of government employment."[5]

The Brookings Institution began as a modest component of the progressive movement of the early twentieth century. A wealthy St. Louis merchant, Robert Brookings,[6] established an Institute of Government Research in 1916 to promote "good government," fight "bossism," assist in municipal reform, and press for economy and efficiency in government. The first major policy decision of the Brookings Institution was the establishment of an annual federal budget. Before 1921, Congress considered appropriation requests individually as they came from various departments and agencies. But the Brookings Institution proposed, and Congress passed, the Budget and Accounting Act of 1921, which created for the first time an integrated federal budget prepared in the Executive Office of the President and presented to Congress in a single budget message. This notable achievement was consistent with the early interests of the Brookings trustees in improving economy and efficiency in government.

The Brookings Institution assumed its present name in 1927, with another large gift from Robert Brookings, as well as donations from Carnegie, Rockefeller, and Eastman (Kodak). Over the years the Institution broke away from being "a sanctuary for conservatives" and recruited a staff of in-house liberal intellectuals. The funds for this effort came mainly from the Ford Foundation. The leadership of the Ford Foundation and the Brookings Institution became closely interlocked.

By the 1960s, Brookings had come to dominate the formulation of national domestic policy. Virtually all of the early planning for President Lyndon B. Johnson's "Great Society" came out of Brookings—including the Economic Opportunity Act 1964; the "War on Poverty"; the establishment of the Medicare and Medicaid programs; the Elementary and Secondary Education Act of 1965, the first large-scale federal aid to education; HeadStart, the popular, federally supported preschool program; and the national Food Stamp program. And despite the election of Republican Richard Nixon in 1968, Brookings continued to oversee the growth of these programs. Brookings personnel regularly rotated into and out of key government posts. In the early 1970s, Brookings developed a proposal for a new congressional budget process and a new Congressional Budget Office. Congress obligingly enacted the Congressional Budget and Impoundment Control Act of 1974, establishing these new budgetary procedures and creating new and powerful House and Senate Budget Committees, with a new joint Congressional Budget Office, headed not unsurprisingly by a Brookings scholar, Alice Rivlin.

But the failure of many of the Great Society programs to bring about their expected results led to a partial breakdown elite consensus during the 1980s on behalf of government intervention to solve social problems. Increasingly, elites began to listen to "neoconservative" scholars and channel resources to newer think tanks (such as the American Enterprise Institute and the Heritage Foundation). Brookings experienced a modest eclipse in power and influence in the 1980s. Moreover, the disastrous economic performance of the late 1970s—high inflation, high unemployment, and low productivity—brought discredit to the Keynesian economic theories that prevailed at Brookings. Brookings's influence was minimal during the Reagan-Bush years.

The Clinton administration provided an opportunity for Brookings to reassert its influence in policy formulation. Brookings scholars went back into government posts, and within the Institution itself, planning began on the Clinton tax-increase and deficit-reduction legislation enacted in 1993. (Brookings scholars were also influential participants in developing Hillary Clinton's unsuccessful comprehensive health care package.) Brookings economists were successful in helping to marshal support for the North American Free Trade Agreement.

Currently, Brookings appears to be focusing its efforts on the development of long-range reform of the Social Security system. And Clinton's policies for the use of the federal government's new revenue surpluses—opposition to tax cuts, support for investment in Social Security, and support for more government spending in education and child care—closely corresponds to Brookings's recommendations. In foreign policy, Brookings strongly supports internationalism and globalism, and its recommendations parallel those of the Council on Foreign Relations.

The American Enterprise Institute

For many years, Republicans dreamed of a "Brookings Institution for Republicans" which would help to offset the liberal Democratic influence of the Brookings Institution. In the late 1970s, moderate elites turn to a previously unknown organization, the American Enterprise Association, which had been founded in 1943 by the Johns-Manville Corporation. Renamed the American Enterprise Institute (AEI) and supported by more conservative foundations (including the Scaife, Bradley, and Olin Foundations), AEI began to assert some influence in developing neoconservative alternatives to the prevailing liberal consensus.

AEI appealed to both Democrats and Republicans who were beginning to have doubts about big government solutions to the nation's social and economic problems. Indeed, AEI distinguished itself from Brookings as follows:

> In confronting social problems those who tend to gravitate to the AEI orbit would be inclined to look first for a market solution . . . while in the other orbit people have a tendency to look for a government solution.[7]

AEI rose quickly in power influence in Washington during the Reagan Administration. It began to set the agenda for policy discussions—tax reductions, deregulation, crime fighting, welfare dependency, and increased defense spending. Even during the Reagan years, however, AEI never quite matched the power of the Brookings Institution in the 1960s and 1970s. Neither the Reagan nor Bush administrations relied directly on AEI to devise programs or write legislation. Instead, AEI's influence came to rest on the high quality of its policy research. Its flagship bimonthly, *The American Enterprise,* publishes some of the best articles on public policy in a lively and engaging style and format. Arguably, AEI's books and reports set the nation's standard for policy work.

Nonetheless, policy work by AEI scholars laid the groundwork for the Welfare Reform Act of 1996. This work convinced many Democrats as well as Republicans in Congress that federal welfare entitlement programs, notably Aid to Families with Dependent Children, were contributing to family breakdown and welfare dependency. Welfare reform generally followed AEI-sponsored recommendations to eliminate the federal entitlement to cash aid, return welfare policymaking to the states, set limits on the length of time that people could be on welfare, and require teenage mothers to stay with their parents and in school is a condition of receiving cash aid.

Today, AEI involves itself in the full range of U.S. domestic and foreign policies, with special emphases on trade policy, government regulation, national security, and social welfare issues. Its top priorities include the following:

- Tax reform: Exploring alternatives to the current federal income tax, including a flat tax and a national sales tax
- Social security reform: Transforming Social Security from a government income-transfer program to a private retirement savings program
- Deregulation: Currently focusing on deregulation of the telecommunications, information technology, and banking industries
- Environmental protection: Using private market alternatives as opposed to government "command and control" methods
- Global environmentalism: Opposition to the surrender of U.S. sovereignty over environmental issues to international bodies

- Social welfare reform: Continuing welfare and Medicaid reforms under the Welfare Reform Act of 1996

Currently AEI boasts of a resident staff of fifty scholars and an annual budget approaching that of the Brookings Institution.

The Heritage Foundation

Influential conservative elites came to understand that without an institutional base in Washington, their influence in the policy formulation process would remain limited. Conservative estrangement from policymaking in Washington was captured in a statement from the Heritage Foundation:

> In those days [1975] . . . we were considered irrelevant by the "opinion-makers" in the media, and the power-brokers in the Congress ignored us. . . . A conservative "think tank," they said, was a contradiction in terms; conservatives had no ideas. History, of course, has proven them wrong.[8]

So they set about the task of "building a solid institutional base" by creating the Heritage Foundation.

The initial funding for Heritage came from Colorado beer tycoon Joseph Coors, who was later joined by two drugstore magnates, Jack Eckerd of Florida and Lewis Lehrman of New York. The Richard Mellon Scaife and John M. Olin Foundations have provided continuing financial support to Heritage over the years.

Yet the Heritage Foundation would have been unlikely to win much influence in Washington had Ronald Reagan not been elected president. Heritage boasts that its 1980 book *Mandate for Leadership* set the policy agenda for the Reagan years. Certainly the foundation helped to publicize that agenda, but there are no specific policy initiatives that can be traced directly to Heritage. At its tenth anniversary banquet in 1984, Reagan himself hailed the foundation as changing "the intellectual history of the West." George Bush was equally extravagant in his praise of Heritage: "You have been real world movers." But these plaudits were designed more to polish the conservative images of the president and vice president than to describe the real influence of Heritage. Of course, Heritage is quite willing to take credit for policies that would have been enacted anyway. Liberals unintentionally cooperate in this image-making by attributing enormous sinister power to Heritage.

The Heritage Foundation "is committed to rolling back the liberal welfare state and building an America where freedom, opportunity, and civil society flourish."[9] Its principal publication, *Policy Review,* has gradually improved in content and quality, so that today it competes favorably with *The American Enterprise* in policy-relevant articles and essays.

Heritage has addressed many of the "hot-button" conservative issues: abortion, racial preferences in affirmative action programs, public vouchers for pupils to attend private religious schools, religion and morality in public life. Yet for the most part, politicians in Washington and in the states have given little more than rhetorical support for the positions advanced by the Heritage Foundation.

Perhaps Heritage's most important contribution to the policy formulation process will turn out to be its efforts to nourish the development of a network of conservative state and local think tanks throughout the nation. Among the more successful of these "mini think tanks" are the Manhattan Institute in New York City, the Reason Foundation in Los Angeles, the Heartland Institute in Chicago, and the Texas Public Policy Foundation in San Antonio. If, indeed, federalism in the American system is ever revived—if there is a continuing "devolution" of policy responsibilities from the government in Washington to the states—then the strategy of Heritage to create a network of policy planning organizations throughout the states may prove farsighted.

THE CONSERVATIVE POLICY NETWORK

When Hillary Clinton complained that a "vast right-wing conspiracy" was behind the effort to impeach her husband, she no doubt had in mind the network of conservative foundations, think tanks, civic and cultural organizations, media outlets, and university-based programs that have arisen in recent years to advance conservative policy ideas. The conservative policy network (see figure 3.2) is far less moneyed and influential than the long-established liberal foundations and think tanks, such as Ford, Rockefeller, Carnegie, MacArthur, and Brookings. Nevertheless, it has succeeded in creating new policy agendas in social welfare, federal entitlements, privatization of public functions, charter schools and vouchers, deregulation, market approaches to environmental protection, community policing and prison building, devolution of policy responsibilities to the states, and the content of television and motion picture productions.

The principal funding of the conservative policy network comes from five sources: the Scaife Foundations, headed by billionaire Richard Mellon Scaife; the Lynde and Harry Bradley Foundation in Milwaukee, Wisconsin; the John M. Olin Foundation; the Koch Family Foundations, headed by oil magnates David and Charles Koch; and the Adolph Coors Foundation, established by Colorado beer mogul Joseph Coors.

Scaife Family Foundations

Richard Mellon Scaife is the great-grandnephew and inheritor of the riches of one of the founders of America's steel industry, Andrew Mellon. The Mellon family fortunes remain tied to USX (formerly United States Steel), Mellon Bank and Trust, and Alcoa. According to former House Speaker Newt Gingrich, Scaife "really created modern conservatism." Scaife was an early and heavy contributor to GOPAC, the political fund that helped make Gingrich Speaker of the House

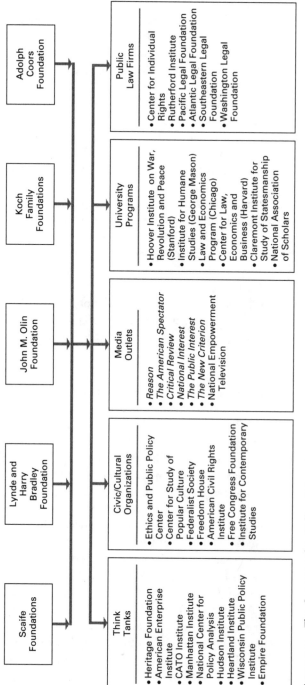

Figure 3.2 The Conservative Policy Network

The figure shows a flow chart. Across the top are five foundations:

- Scaife Foundations
- Lynde and Harry Bradley Foundation
- John M. Olin Foundation
- Koch Family Foundations
- Adolph Coors Foundation

These feed into five categories of organizations:

Think Tanks
- Heritage Foundation
- American Enterprise Institute
- CATO Institute
- Manhattan Institute
- National Center for Policy Analysis
- Hudson Institute
- Heartland Institute
- Wisconsin Public Policy Institute
- Empire Foundation

Civic/Cultural Organizations
- Ethics and Public Policy Center
- Center for Study of Popular Culture
- Federalist Society
- Freedom House
- American Civil Rights Institute
- Free Congress Foundation
- Institute for Contemporary Studies

Media Outlets
- *Reason*
- *The American Spectator*
- *Critical Review*
- *National Interest*
- *The Public Interest*
- *The New Criterion*
- National Empowerment Television

University Programs
- Hoover Institute on War, Revolution and Peace (Stanford)
- Institute for Humane Studies (George Mason)
- Law and Economics Program (Chicago)
- Center for Law, Economics and Business (Harvard)
- Claremont Institute for Study of Statesmanship
- National Association of Scholars

Public Law Firms
- Center for Individual Rights
- Rutherford Institute
- Pacific Legal Foundation
- Atlantic Legal Foundation
- Southeastern Legal Foundation
- Washington Legal Foundation

in 1994. His foundations (Sarah Scaife Foundation, Scaife Family Foundation, Carthage Foundation, and Allegheny Foundation) have contributed large sums to a variety of organizations, including the Heritage Foundation, the American Enterprise Institute, and the Hoover Institute on War, Revolution and Peace at Stanford University. His Allegheny Foundation has given millions to his hometown Pittsburgh's redevelopment.

But it was Scaife's bankrolling of several organizations involved in the movement to impeach President Bill Clinton that won him the enmity of Hillary Clinton. Scaife contributed heavily to the magazine *American Spectator* and its "Arkansas Project" that began the investigation into Clinton's early sexual indiscretions. Scaife is a major benefactor of the public policy school at Pepperdine University—the school that offered Independent Counsel Kenneth Starr a plush deanship that he intended to take after Clinton's impeachment but was forced by bad publicity to turn down. It was a reporter on a Scaife-owned Pittsburgh newspaper who published the book *The Strange Death of Vincent Foster*, suggesting that the White House counselor and close friend of Hillary may have been murdered. Scaife money also found its way to the once-little-known Rutherford Institute that provided the funding for Paula Jones to bring her suit for sexual harassment against Bill Clinton while he was governor of Arkansas. It is doubtful that Clinton would have been impeached by the U.S. House of Representatives without the resources supplied by Richard Mellon Scaife.

Bradley Foundation

The Lynde and Harry Bradley Foundation has skillfully directed its limited resources to advance conservative policy initiatives. (Brothers Lynde and Harry made their fortune in electronic and radio components and then sold their successful corporation to Rockwell International, the aerospace and defense industry conglomerate.) The foundation was instrumental in creating the first public educational school voucher program in its hometown, Milwaukee. The Milwaukee program has now become the model for the school voucher movement throughout the nation. Bradley was also an early major sponsor of National Empowerment Television (NET), the conservative movement's cable television outlet.

The Bradley Foundation publicly laments the flow of authority in the nation "toward centralized, bureaucratic, service-providing institutions" that treat citizens as "clients." It seeks to "reinvigorate and reempower the traditional, local institutions—families, school, churches, and neighborhoods." In addition to heavy support of the American Enterprise Institute and the Heritage Foundation in Washington, Bradley has attempted to fund a variety of state-level conservative think tanks, including the Hudson Institute (Indiana), the Manhattan Institute (New York), the Heartland Institute (Illinois), and the Wisconsin Policy Research Institute. Bradley also funds conservative scholars through fellowship grants that it offers to both think tanks and universities: Bradley Fellows are funded at the Ethics and Public Policy Center in Washington, George Mason University, Georgetown University, Harvard University, the Heritage Foundation, Michigan State University, New York University, Stanford University, the University of Chicago, and the University of Wisconsin–Milwaukee, among others. The Bradley Foundation also helps support the National Association of Scholars in its nationwide effort to organize college and university faculty to fight "political correctness" on campus.

Bradley has also funded individual scholars who have produced influential books on public policy. It funded Charles Murray's book *Losing Ground,* which helped to inspire the welfare reform movement, and his coauthored controversial book *The Bell Curve,* which argues among other things that efforts to train and educate the least intelligent people in society are bound to fail.

John M. Olin Foundation

The John M. Olin Foundation has attempted to sponsor a conservative presence at some of the nation's leading universities. Olin's president, William Simon, the former Secretary of the Treasury in the Reagan administration, has urged his elite colleagues in business and finance to stop "financing left-wing intellectuals and institutions which espouse the exact opposite of what they believe in."

The Olin Foundation has been instrumental in the development of "Law and Economics" programs in universities throughout the nation. These programs emphasize free-market economics as it applies to law. Olin-supported programs exist at the University of Chicago, Harvard University, George Mason University, and Yale University, among others. The foundation also helps to sponsor the Federalist Society, an association of conservative law school students.

Olin, like Bradley, also funds the work of selected conservative scholars. Olin Fellowships supported Allan Bloom's influential *The Closing of the American Mind,* a devastating critique of America's declining cultural and intellectual standards; Dinesh D'Souza's *The End of Racism,* arguing that affirmative action programs are no longer necessary; and the work of the conservative movement's unsuccessful nominee for the U.S. Supreme Court, Robert Bork, including *The Tempting of America,* an argument that the Constitution has been undermined by political forces that create new "rights" for their own advantage.

Koch Family Foundations

Koch Industries, an oil, natural gas, and land management company, is one of the largest privately owned companies in America. Three family foundations are operated by the Kochs (the Charles G. Koch, David H. Koch, and Claude R. Lambe Foundations). These foundations constitute the principal financial backing for the libertarian movement in America.

The major beneficiary of the Koch foundations has been the CATO Institute, a small think tank committed to libertarian ideas. It came to Washington in 1981 as an offspring of the Libertarian Party but gradually entered mainstream policy debates with free-market, limited-government, and antiregulatory studies and recommendations. (It is named for *Cato's Letters,* libertarian pamphlets that were distributed in the American colonies in the early 1700s and played a major role in laying the philosophical foundation for the American Revolution.) According to the CATO Institute, "A pervasive intolerance for individual rights is shown by government's arbitrary intrusion into private economic transactions and its disregard for civil liberties." True to its own beliefs, the institute accepts no government funding.

Mainstream conservatives generally applaud CATO's efforts to free the economy from government intervention and reduce taxes and the size of government. But they cringe at CATO's positions on social policy, for example, its call to legalize drugs. CATO also opposes spending for national defense and foreign aid, and it urges a general withdrawal of United States from world politics. It publishes the *CATO Policy Review* as well as the more scholarly *CATO Journal.*

The Koch Foundations also support *Reason* magazine, a media outlet for libertarian ideas, as well as the Institute for Justice, a libertarian public interest law firm in Washington. It also channels funds into grants and fellowships for conservative university programs, notably the Institute for Humane Studies at George Mason University.

Adolph Coors Foundation

The Adolph Coors brewing company of Colorado was founded in 1873 by Adolph Coors Sr., and it has remained a family-owned company since then. The Adolph Coors Foundation, headed by descendants Joseph and William Coors, emerged in the 1970s as a major source of funding for the conservative policy agenda.

The initial funding for the establishment of the Heritage Foundation came in 1973 from Joseph Coors; he was assisted in this effort by two drugstore magnets, Jack Eckerd of Florida and Lewis I. Lehrman of New York. They were not satisfied with the more moderate neoconservatism of the American Enterprise Institute. They deliberately recruited younger and more passionate writers to Heritage. They wanted a think tank that would be "on top of the news" and always ready to provide a quick "backgrounder" for reporters.

Heritage boasts that its *Mandate for Leadership* report in 1980 was the blueprint for the Reagan administration, that Reagan's early policy successes were "primarily due to the fact that his script had already been written for him by the Heritage Foundation before he won the election."

It was Coors Foundation money that helped to underwrite the successful effort to thwart the Equal Rights Amendment (ERA). The foundation was a major supporter of Phyllis Schlafly's Eagle Forum, which led the opposition in the states to the ratification of the ERA. The foundation has also provided major funding for Accuracy in Media, an organization formed to combat liberal bias in the media, and for the Free Congress Foundation, an active ideological interest group in Washington, D.C.

GLOBAL THINKING: THE COUNCIL ON FOREIGN RELATIONS AND THE TRILATERAL COMMISSION

The global economy requires a global elite. The Council on Foreign Relations and its multinational extension, the Trilateral Commission, have become truly "global think tanks," developing global policies and promoting interaction among global elites. The Council on Foreign Relations (CFR) has long been at the center of U.S. foreign policy formulation. The Trilateral Commission is an outgrowth of the CFR. It is the world's first global policy planning organization with elite members from Japan, Western Europe, and the United States.

The Council on Foreign Relations

The most influential policy planning group in foreign affairs is the Council on Foreign Relations. The origins of the CFR go back to the Versailles Treaty in 1919 ending World War I. Some Americans, including Woodrow Wilson's key adviser, Edward M. House, believed that top leadership in the United States was not sufficiently informed about world affairs. The Council on Foreign Relations was founded in 1921 and was supported by grants from the Rockefeller and Carnegie Foundations and later the Ford Foundation.

The CFR's mission is to develop foreign policy directions and build consensus for them among the nation's elite. It initiates new policy directions by first commissioning scholars to undertake investigations of foreign policy questions. Its studies are usually made with the financial support of foundations. Upon their completion, the CFR holds seminars and discussions among its members and between its members and top government officials.

CFR publishes the journal *Foreign Affairs,* considered throughout the world to be the unofficial mouthpiece of U.S. foreign policy. Few important initiatives in U.S. policy have not been first outlined in articles in this publication. (It was in *Foreign Affairs* in 1947 that George F. Kennan, chief of the policy planning staff of the State Department, writing under the pseudonym of "X," first announced U.S. intentions of "containing" communist expansion in the world.)

The history of CFR policy accomplishments is dazzling. It developed the Kellogg Peace Pact in the 1920s, stiffened U.S. opposition to Japanese Pacific expansion in the 1930s, designed major portions of the United Nations' charter, and devised the containment policy to halt Soviet expansion in Europe after World War II. It also laid the groundwork for the NATO agreement and devised the Marshall Plan for European recovery. In the Kennedy and Johnson administrations, the council took the lead in formulating U.S. policy in Southeast Asia—including both the initial decision to intervene militarily in Vietnam and the later decision to withdraw.

In 1968, following the bloody Vietnamese Tet offensive study, the CFR launched a new study group, the "Vietnam Settlement Group," headed by Wall Street investment banker Robert V. Roosa and Wall Street lawyer Cyrus Vance. The group devised a peace proposal allowing for the return of prisoners and a standstill ceasefire, with the Viet Cong and Saigon dividing the territory under their respective controls. Secretary of State Henry Kissinger avoided directly attributing U.S. policy to the CFR plan, but the plan itself eventually became the basis of the January 1973 Paris Peace Agreement, ending U.S. participation in the Vietnam War.

Following Vietnam, the CFR, under David Rockefeller's tenure as chairman, began its 1980s Project. This was an ambitious program even for so powerful a group as the CFR. But money from the Ford, Lilly, Mellon, and Rockefeller Foundations provided the necessary resources. The project officially began in 1975 and lasted until 1980, and it included an international campaign on behalf of human rights; an effort to restrict international arms sales; and a study of "North-South global relations"—relations between richer and poorer countries. Upon taking office in 1977, the Carter administration set all of these policies in motion. It restricted international arms sales; it encouraged private and World Bank loans to less developed countries; and, most important, it initiated a worldwide human rights campaign in which U.S. trade and aid were curtailed in countries that did not live up to human rights standards.

But the CFR itself, still under Rockefeller's direction, gradually became aware of the crumbling foreign and military policies of the United States during the Carter administration. In 1980, the CFR issued a stern report citing "sharp anguish over Americans held hostage by international outlaws" (Iran) and "the brutal invasion of a strategic nation" (Afghanistan). It described U.S. defenses as "a troubling question."[10] More important, the CFR announced the end of the 1980s Project, with its concern for human rights, and initiated a new study program on U.S.-Soviet relations. Even before Carter left office, leading CFR members had decided that the human rights policy was crippling U.S. relations with its allies but was not affecting policies in communist countries. Moreover, the CFR recognized "the relentless Soviet military buildup and extension of power by invasion, opportunism, and proxy," and recommended that the U.S.-Soviet relationship "occupy center stage in the coming decade." Thus, elite support for a harder line in foreign policy and a rebuilding of America's defenses had been developed through the CFR even before Ronald Reagan took office.

The CFR announced its new hard line toward the Soviet Union in a 1981 report, *The Soviet Challenge: A Policy Framework for the 1980s*. It recommended a comprehensive, long-term military buildup by the United States, and it even argued that arms control should no longer be the "centerpiece of U.S. policy toward the Soviets." It also recommended that the United States be prepared to use force in unstable areas of the world, such as the Persian Gulf.

The Reagan administration, like those that preceded it, relied heavily on CFR advice. However, because of some conservative objections to the "internationalism" of the Council on Foreign Relations, CFR members on the Reagan team did not publicize their membership. Indeed, during the 1980 campaign, CFR and Trilateral Commission member George Bush was forced to resign from both organizations to deflect right-wing attacks that he was part of the CFR "conspiracy" to subvert U.S. interests to an "international government."

The CFR takes pride in the success of the Cold War containment policy that was first outlined by member George Kennan in his 1947 "X" article in *Foreign Affairs.* But it recognizes that the end of the Cold War necessitates a restructuring of fundamental policy goals. It seeks "to formulate a new organizing principle for American activities overseas in place of the East-West paradigm of the Cold War."[11] Above all, the CFR seeks to keep the United States actively involved in international politics, that is, to avoid isolationism, trade barriers, and xenophobia. Its members actively support U.S. aid to Russia and other former Soviet republics, the North Atlantic Free Trade Agreement and other efforts to stimulate global trade, an active U.S. role in peace efforts in the Middle East and in the republics of the former Yugoslavia, and the development of a strategy for dealing with the Islamic world.

The current chairman of the CFR is Wall Street investment banker Peter G. Peterson. Among the CFR's current major areas of research focus is the continuing development of the global economy (see "The Globalization of Economic Power" in chapter 2, p. 20). In addition, the CFR is "rethinking national security"—trying to develop policies to cope with the growing availability throughout the world of biological, chemical, and nuclear weapons.[12]

The Trilateral Commission

The Trilateral Commission was created in 1973 "to foster closer cooperation among these principal democratic industrialized areas [Japan, Western Europe, and the United States] with shared leadership responsibilities in the wider international system."[13] The commission was originally established by the Council on Foreign Relations Chairman David Rockefeller with the support of the council and the Rockefeller Foundation. In explaining why the Trilateral Commission was formed, Rockefeller, in typically condescending elitist language, stated:

> Governments don't have time to think about the broader longer-range issues. It seemed to make sense to persuade a group of private, qualified citizens to get together to identify the key issues affecting the world and possible solutions.[14]

The Trilateral Commission has played a major role in virtually every important international agreement involving the industrialized democracies over the

MEETING ON PROPOSED TRILATERAL COMMISSION
Pocantico, N.Y., July 23-24, 1972

Present were: Messrs. C. Fred Bergsten, Robert Bowie, Zbigniew Brzezinski,
     McGeorge Bundy, Karl Carstens, Guido Colonna di Paliano,
     François Duchene, René Foch, Max Kohnstamm, Bayless Manning,
     Kiichi Miyazawa, Kinhide Mushakoji, Saburo Okita, Henry Owen,
     Tadashi Yamamoto (observer), David Rockefeller (Acting Chairman),
     George Franklin (Secretary, pro tem).
     S. Frederick Starr, Edward Morse, Rapporteurs.

     Mr. Rockefeller welcomed the participants. He expressed his con-
cern over the impact of growing economic competitiveness and the accel-
erating pace of technological and social change on policy-making in major
industrialized states. At a time when such transformations make it
imperative that governments devote more attention to the problems of the
future, they are compelled instead to concentrate more than ever on
issues of the moment. In such circumstances, he felt, there is danger
that the advanced industrialized states will drift aimlessly into a
situation in which they may inflict harm upon each other and other states.
Now is a propitious time for persons from the private sector to make a
valuable contribution to public policy. This could be accomplished, Mr.

Commission to-be...

Rockefeller suggested, if individuals from the academic communities,
labor and religious groups, as well as business, were to join together
to consider neglected longer-term issues and to translate their conclusions
into practical policy recommendations.

     He also reviewed discussions concerning such an international com-
mission held with Japanese leaders, with United States officials, including
Mr. Henry Kissinger, and with many participants in the present meeting. All
had been strongly encouraging.

     He also reviewed discussions concerning such an international com-
mission held with Japanese leaders, with United States officials, including
Mr. Henry Kissinger, and with many participants in the present meeting. All
had been strongly encouraging.

7

Actual Minutes of First Trilateral Commission Meeting

past three decades. The first contribution of the commission was the initiation
of regular economic summit meetings between the heads of the Western European nations, the United States, and Japan. These economic summits, with the
support of national elites and the Trilateral Commission, in turn advanced the
global economy through the European Union, the General Agreement on Tariffs

and Trade, the World Bank, and the International Monetary Fund. (See feature: "Deciding on Global Trade Policy," pp. 27–29.)

The Trilateral Commission proclaims itself to be a nongovernmental organization. It boasts of drawing together "the highest level unofficial group possible."[15] Its membership consists of more than 300 "distinguished individuals" from each of the three regions—Western Europe, United States, and Japan. The work of the commission generally involves teams of authors from the three regions working together for a year or more on draft reports, which are then discussed at the annual meeting of the commission and later published as "Triangle Papers." In addition, each regional group within the commission carries out some activities on its own.

The current North American chairman of the Trilateral Commission is Paul A. Volcker, former chairman of the Board of Governors of the U.S. Federal Reserve System. (David Rockefeller currently holds the title "Founder and Honorary Chairman.") Some titles from recent Triangle Papers indicate the current concerns of the commission: *Managing the International System over the Next Ten Years; Globalization and Trilateral Labor Markets;* and *Maintaining Energy Security in a Global Context.*

COORDINATING ELITE POLICY FORMULATION

The elite institutions of policy formulation—the leading foundations, the influential think tanks, the global policy-planning organizations—form a loose policy network. But there is no central direction to this network, no imposed unity of viewpoints, no all-powerful hidden conspiracy. There are, however, a variety of deliberate efforts at elite consensus-building and coordination of policy formulation. These efforts are reflected in discussion groups, task forces, councils, and roundtables that bring together top leaders from the corporate and financial worlds, the foundations and think tanks, the mass media, and the government itself. Indeed, certain elite institutions—notably the Business Roundtable and the Council on Economic Development—were created specifically to help bring about elite consensus on major policy issues.

The Council on Economic Development

The Council on Economic Development (CED) was founded by the nation's top corporate and financial elites during World War II with the goal of shaping the postwar world. The CED takes credit for the formulation of the Marshall Plan that help bring about the economic recovery of Western Europe after the war. It was instrumental in the formulation of the Full Employment Act of 1946 which, among other things, established the President's Council of Economic Advisers and the Joint Economic Committee of Congress. The CED took the early lead in encouraging economic globalization—shaping the Bretton Woods Agreement that led to the creation of the World Bank and the International

Monetary Fund. The CED worked closely with the Council on Foreign Relations in the creation of these international organizations.

The CED describes itself as "an independent, nonpartisan organization of business and education leaders dedicated to policy research on the major economic and social issues of our time." Its Board of Trustees is composed of more than 200 executives of major U.S. corporations together with a small contingent of university presidents. The trustees organize and oversee the work of many policy-specific committees as well as the organization's staff in New York—deciding what policy issues CED will address, reviewing the progress of its "policy projects," and approving official CED policy statements. Recently, the board has approved policy statements in support of welfare reform, limiting the regulatory authority of federal agencies, and tort reform—limiting corporate liability for defective products.

CED does more than formulate policy. It also functions as a business interest group in Washington, D.C. It does so despite its own denial that it engages in lobbying activity: "CED Trustees do not lobby, but they promote CED's stated positions through such activities as congressional testimony and one-on-one briefings with top government officials."[16]

The CED may have lost influence in recent years, both as a coordinating and consensus-building institution among elites, and as a defender of corporate interests in Washington, D.C. The CED does not appear to have been directly responsible for any significant new policy changes in recent years. Its efforts to reduce the regulatory authority of the Environmental Protection Agency, the Food and Drug Administration, the Occupational Safety and Health Administration, and so forth, have largely failed. Its efforts at tort reform have been effectively checked by the nation's powerful legal community—the Washington law firms, the American Bar Association, the American Trial Lawyers Association, as well as the many lawyers who served in Congress themselves. But even more convincing evidence of CED's waning influence may be inferred from examining the membership of its Board of Trustees. No longer are the *heads* of top corporations and banks represented among the trustees, that is, the chairman and chief executive officers (CEOs). Instead, the trustees appear to be vice presidents of larger corporations and CEOs of smaller firms.

The Business Roundtable

Currently the Business Roundtable appears to be the most prominent elite coordinating institution. It is an active association of the chief executive officers of the nation's 200 largest corporations, including manufacturing, banking, insurance, retail, transportation, and media corporations. The power of the Business Roundtable stems in part from its "firm rule" that a corporate chieftain cannot send a substitute to its meetings. In the words of the Roundtable itself: "The participation of the Chief Executive is the distinguishing feature of the Roundtable."[17] Vice presidents are not welcome.

The Business Roundtable was established in 1972 "in the belief that business executives should take an increased role in the continuing debates about public policy." Of course, business already had a powerful role in Washington policymaking through such organizations as the U.S. Chamber of Commerce, the National Association of Manufacturers, the Business Council, and hundreds of industry associations such as the American Bankers Association, American Petroleum Institute, and American Iron and Steel Institute. So why create a superorganization? The Business Roundtable itself says:

> The answer is that business leaders believed . . . [that] they wanted an organization in which the Chief Executive Officers of leading corporations take positions and advocate those positions.[18]

In short, traditional interest-group representation was considered inadequate for the nation's *top* corporate leaders. They wished to come together *themselves* to decide on policy issues and press their views in Washington. (See chapter 5 for a review of the Business Roundtable's lobbying efforts.)

The Roundtable's policy formulation and coordination is done by its "Task Forces." Each is headed by a prominent corporate CEO and has only CEOs as its members. Each focuses on a specific policy area, conducting studies, developing a consensus on policy directions, and laying out plans for implementing its recommendations. Implementation often involves testifying before congressional committees as well as making personal contact with government decision makers. Currently there are Task Forces on corporate governance, education, environment, federal budget, government regulation, health and retirement, international trade investment, taxation, and tort reform.

The Untidiness of Policy Formulation

The policy formulation process is not always as neat as our diagram (figure 3.1, p. 40) suggests. Elite policy formulation is often untidy, disorderly, and uncoordinated. Elites frequently disagree, especially over the details of policy initiatives. Foundations sometimes fund studies that make conflicting policy recommendations, and think tanks compete with one another for preeminence in policymaking. But interelite conflict and competition takes place within a broader consensus on the goals of public policy, especially economic growth, global expansion, and the protection of corporate enterprise.

"The staid and dignified policy-formation process is very different from the helter-skelter special-interest process. . . . It appears as disinterested and fair-minded as the special-interest process seems self-seeking and biased."[19] The foundations, think tanks, and policy planning organizations generally try to remain above partisan politics. Their tax-exempt status under Section 501c3 of the Internal Revenue Code requires that they remain nonpartisan, that they do not endorse political candidates, and that their policy recommendations be presented as "civic and educational" activities. They describe themselves as "independent," "nonpartisan," "objective," "problem-solving," and "public-spirited."

Collectively, the organizations active in the policy formulation process perform a variety of important functions for the nation's elite. They provide settings for top leadership to familiarize themselves with policy issues; to listen to policy experts in seminars and briefings; to ensure that they receive the latest and best information on policy issues; and to encourage compromise and consensus building. And these organizations provide the institutional framework for defining social problems and determining national priorities; for funding research on policy directions and solutions; and for communicating elite concerns and recommendations to government decision makers.

CHAPTER 4

The Leadership Selection Process

There are two things that are important in politics. The first is money and I can't remember what the second one is.
— U.S. SENATOR MARK HANNA (1895)

Ready money is a candidate's best friend.
— U.S. SENATOR PHIL GRAMM (1995)

MONEY DOMINATES THE process of selecting America's political leadership. No one can seriously contend for high public office in the United States without access to big money sources to finance a campaign.

Professional political campaigns, with their heavy reliance on television advertising, are very costly. These high costs force *all* candidates—Democrats and Republicans, liberals and conservatives—to turn to big money sources to fund their quests for political office. Virtually all candidates for high public office must first appeal to moneyed elites *before* they can even consider appealing to the voters. The only exceptions are those candidates who themselves have enough money to fund their own campaigns. Elites provide financial support for both political parties, and they often even provide financial support for opposing candidates in the same election, ensuring that elites themselves seldom if ever lose.

The principal source of money for political campaigns in America is the nation's elite—the same corporations, banks, law and investment firms, media conglomerates, and wealthy individuals who dominate the policymaking process. Indeed, their dominance in political campaign finances provides yet another means by which they can ensure that their own preferences and interests are protected by elected office-holders and reflected in public policy.

TOP-DOWN LEADERSHIP SELECTION

Serious candidates for elected office in America must *begin* their "exploratory" efforts by contacting moneyed elites even before they decide to declare themselves as candidates. If aspiring candidates fail to receive credible pledges of financial assistance in advance of opening their campaigns, they are well advised by professional campaign managers to forget about their current political aspirations. Even lukewarm early responses by big money sources are regarded as a clear signal to aspirants to leave the race to others. Serious candidates must have dollars in hand to open their campaigns as well as credible assurances of a continuing flow of contributions throughout the campaign.

To win the necessary financial support of moneyed elites, candidates must convince them of their personal agreement with the values and interests of elites and their willingness to work to ensure that these values and interests are reflected in public policy. Elites must also be convinced of a candidate's electability—his or her likelihood of success at the polls. Elites are regularly approached by numerous aspiring politicians who solemnly pledge to support elite interests, but most elites are prudent in their political investments. They do not like to back losers.

Elites can direct their campaign contributions through a number of separate channels (see figure 4.1). Individuals may contribute *directly to campaign funds* of candidates. These contributions, however, are subject to limits enforced by the Federal Election Commission: $1,000 to any candidate by any individual per election. Of course, there are many ways that individual contributors can legally surmount this limit. For example, contributors may give a candidate $1,000 for each member of their family in a primary election and then another $1,000 per member in the general election. Nonetheless, these modest limits on the direct flow of money to candidates' campaign chests have led to a variety of other important channels of cash flow.

No limits are placed on the size of contributions made to *political parties.* Technically, this "soft money" is supposed to be used for party building, get-out-the-vote drives, issue education, and general party participation. In reality, both parties spend this money directly in support of their candidates for public office. Indeed, these party contributions are often earmarked for the candidates who were responsible for raising them. Thus, for example, if a major contributor wishes to donate $10,000, $25,000, or $100,000 to a candidate, he or she writes out the check to the Democratic or Republican national or state committee, with the unwritten understanding that the party will spend that money on the contributor's preferred candidate.

Soft money is the fastest growing source of campaign funds (see table 4.2, p. 70). Nearly all soft money is raised in large contributions—indeed, the reason soft money is becoming so popular is that it allows big donors to give money without being obliged to abide by the limits imposed on direct campaign contributions. Another advantage is that corporations and labor unions can write checks directly from their organization's treasury, which they cannot do for direct contributions to candidates.

Political action committees (PACs) were initially invented by labor unions as a way to evade limits on their direct contributions to political candidates. But today PACs are organized not only by unions, but also corporations, trade and

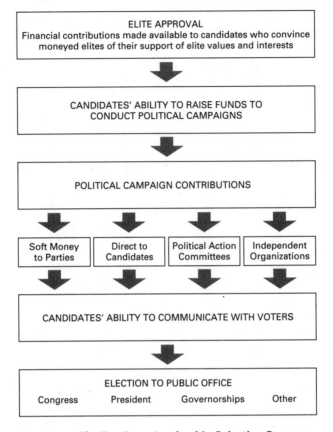

Figure 4.1 The Top-Down Leadership Selection Process

professional associations, environmental organizations, liberal and conservative ideological groups, and virtually every other type of organized interest group in the nation. Individuals associated with these organizations donate to their PACs, which in turn contribute money to the candidates. The distribution of PAC money is determined by the leadership of the interest groups who sponsor the PACs (see chapter 5).

Political candidates can spend as much of their own money on their own campaigns as they wish. The U.S. Supreme Court decided in 1976 in *Buckley* v. *Valeo*[1] that limiting an individual's ability to spend money on his or her own political communications was an unconstitutional infringement of the First Amendment right of free speech.

Spending by individuals and independent organizations to advocate their views on issues or their policy positions is also protected by the Constitution. Federal election law prohibits independent organizations from directly endorsing candidates in paid advertising. But these organizations cannot be prohibited from setting forth their views during a campaign, even if those views closely correspond to the campaign issues advocated by a candidate. The only limit on such "issue ads" is that they are not supposed to be coordinated with a party or a candidate's campaign organization. Spending for issue ads has grown exponentially in recent election cycles.

Money has always played an important role in American politics (see feature: "A Brief History of Money in Politics," pp. 72–73). But the cost of getting elected to high office today greatly magnifies the political influence of monied elites.

THE COSTS OF GETTING ELECTED

The influence of the moneyed elite has been vastly increased by the high and rising costs of political campaigns in recent years (see figure 4.2). Campaign spending in a presidential election—including spending by *all* presidential and congressional candidates, *both* political parties, *and* independent political organizations—now exceeds $3 billion! The most important hurdle for any candidate for public office is raising funds to meet campaign costs.

Fund-raising occupies more of a candidate's time than any other campaign activity. Candidates must personally contact as many "fat cat" contributors as possible. They must work late each evening on the telephone with potential contributors. They must arrange fund-raising dinners, cocktail parties, and similar events, nearly every day of the campaign. The candidate is expected to appear personally at these events to "press the flesh" of big contributors. Assorted celebrities must be asked to appear to generate attendance. Tickets to these events, ranging in cost from $250 to $1,000, must be "bundled" to be sold in blocks to wealthy contributors, corporations, banks, and other organizations. Fund-raising is the heart of the campaign.

Fund-raising has become the central factor in leadership selection because of the high cost of running for public office. Getting elected has never been more expensive. The cost of the *average* winning campaign for the U.S. House of Representatives is now approaching $1 million: In 1998 the average winner of a House seat spent more than $700,000 (see table 4.1, p. 70). The single most expensive House campaign was that of former Republican Speaker Newt Gingrich at $7.6 million in 1998; and Democratic House Leader Richard Gephardt spent more than $2.5 million in 1996. House candidates, of course, must raise these amounts *every two years*.

Winning a seat in the U.S. Senate now costs an average of about $5 million. Averages mean less in the Senate, however, because the amount required for a Senate campaign varies a great deal from state to state. Interestingly, the biggest Senate campaign spenders in recent elections have been losers: Republican Senator Alfonse D'Amato lost his reelection bid in 1998 despite spending more than

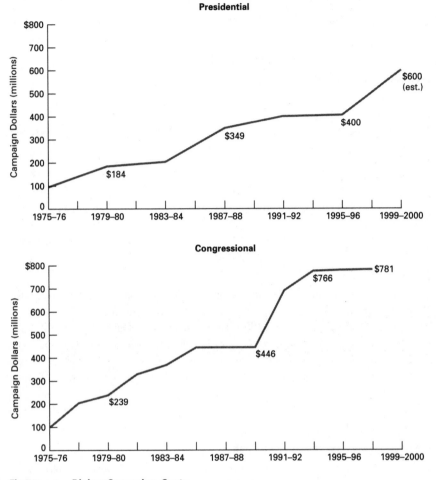

Figure 4.2   Rising Campaign Costs

$24 million, while his successful challenger Democrat Charles Schumer spent only about $17 million; and Michael Huffington spent $30 million in a losing effort in California in 1994.

WHO PAYS FOR ELECTIONS

Campaign funds come from a variety of sources—small donors, big donors, interest groups, corporations, labor unions, and even taxpayers (see table 4.2). In some cases, candidates pay their own way. Typically, however, candidates for high public office—especially incumbents—fund their campaigns using other people's money.

Table 4.1 The Cost of a Seat in Congress

	1998	1996
Senate		
Average winner spent	$5,227,761	$4,692,100
Average loser spent	2,839,813	2,773,756
Most expensive campaign	27,159,681	14,587,143
	(Alfonse D'Amato, R-N.Y.)	(Jesse Helms, R-N.C.)
House of Representatives		
Average winner spent	650,428	673,739
Average loser spent	210,614	265,675
Most expensive campaign	7,578,716	5,577,715
	(Newt Gingrich, R-Ga.)	(Newt Gingrich, R-Ga.)

Source: Federal Election Commission, 1999.

It is true that small donations—donations of less than $200—make up the largest single source of campaign cash, about 30 percent. Virtually all of these donations are hard money contributions—money given directly to candidates' campaign chests and subject to regulatory limits. Yet even these small donations originate primarily from wealthy, upper-class, older, white males with conservative views (see table 4.3). Four-fifths of donors have annual incomes of more than $100,000; more than four-fifths are forty-five years of age or older; and

Table 4.2 Sources of Campaign Cash

Source	PRESIDENTIAL ELECTION YEAR 1996		MIDTERM CONGRESSIONAL ELECTION YEAR 1998	
	Millions of Dollars	Percentage	Millions of Dollars	Percentage
Small donations	734	30.6	351	23.5
Large individual donors	597	21.8	464	31.0
Political action committees	243	10.1	269	18.0
Soft money	262	10.8	225	15.0
Candidates	161	6.7	92	6.1
Public (taxpayer) financing	211	8.8	—	—
Other	200	8.2	95	6.4
Total	2,400	100.0	1,496	100.0

Source: Center for Responsive Politics, from Federal Election Commission data.

Table 4.3   Characteristics of Individual Campaign Contributors (in percentages)

INCOME

More than $500,000	20
More than $100,000	81
Less than $100,000	19
Less than $50,000	5

AGE

Over 60	47
30–60	40
30–45	11
18–30	1

RACE

White	95
Nonwhite	5

SEX

Male	81
Female	19

IDEOLOGY

Strong conservative	10
Conservative	13
Moderate leaning conservative	28
Moderate	19
Moderate leaning liberal	10
Liberal	18
Strong liberal	3

CONTACT WITH CONGRESS MEMBERS (DURING PAST TWO YEARS)

	House	Senate
None	27	22
Once	22	16
More than once	51	51

Source: John Green, Paul Herrnson, Lynda Powell, Clyde Wilcox, "Individual Congressional Campaign Contributions," press release, 9 June 1998, Center for Responsive Politics.

about half identify themselves as conservatives, while only one-third identify themselves as liberals. More important, more than two-thirds of these small donors contacted at least one member of the House of Representatives or Senate over a two-year period.

FEATURE: A BRIEF HISTORY OF MONEY IN POLITICS

In 1757, in his race for a seat in the Virginia House of Burgesses, George Washington was reprimanded for purchasing and distributing more than a quart of whiskey per voter in his district. But for the first fifty years or so of American independence, campaign costs were relatively low. The population was small, and only white males who owned property—about one of every five adults—were allowed to vote. But as the population grew, and property requirements were abolished, campaign costs rose. By 1840 the practice of buying votes was well established in the nation's cities.

Rising campaign costs in the early nineteenth century required candidates to begin soliciting funds from businesses, industries, and wealthy individuals. These contributors, in turn, increasingly sought favors from a government that was becoming more and more involved in economic matters. During the Civil War, Abraham Lincoln wrote:

> As a result of the war, corporations have become enthroned, and an era of corruption in high places will follow. The money power of the country will endeavor to prolong its rule by preying on the prejudices of the people until all wealth is concentrated in a few hands.

During the industrial revolution following the Civil War, historian Richard Hofstadter describes what may have been the high–water mark of corruption in American politics: "Capitalists seeking land grants, tariffs, bounties, favorable currency policies, freedom from regulatory legislation and economic reform, supplied campaign funds, fees, and bribes, and plied politicians with investment opportunities." Banks, railroads, and oil and mining companies became the major sources of campaign cash in national politics; in local politics, campaigns were funded by utilities, saloons, gambling halls, houses of prostitution, and racetracks. According to historian George Thayer, "Standard Oil did everything to the Pennsylvania Legislature except refine it." The presidential election of 1896 set a record for campaign spending that would not be surpassed in equivalent dollars until the 1970s. U.S. Senator Marcus Alonzo Hanna, general counsel for John D. Rockefeller's Standard Oil Company, raised between $6 and $7 million for the winner, Republican William McKinley, while his Democratic opponent William Jennings Bryan spent only about a half million dollars.

Political campaign costs rose again following the Seventeenth Amendment (1913), which instituted the direct election of U.S. senators; the nineteenth Amendment, which won women the right to vote; and the expanding use of primary elections to choose party candidates. Fortunately for politicians who began to need more campaign money to reach more voters, the New Deal vastly increased government involvement in the economy and thereby raised the incentives for business interests to fork over more money to ensure that their interests would be protected in policymaking. Labor unions became a major source of campaign funds in 1936 when the newly formed Congress of Industrial Organizations (CIO) contributed a half million dollars to Franklin D. Roosevelt's presidential campaign.

During the 1950s and 1960s, each of the major parties enjoyed the support of wealthy "superdonors"—the Mellons and Rockefellers on the Republican side and the Kennedys and Harrimans on the Democratic side. But a turning point in campaign finance history occurred after the Watergate revelations of secret donations to the 1972 Nixon reelection campaign, especially the $2 million individual contribution by insurance magnate Clement Stone. The result was the passage of the Federal Election Campaign Act, creating the Federal Elections Commission (FEC) and placing limits on direct campaign contributions to candidates by individuals and organizations.

But the reforms envisioned by the act were quickly undermined by an explosion in the number of political action committees, vast increases in unlimited "soft money" contributions to the parties, and the U.S. Supreme Court decision in *Buckley* v. *Valeo* declaring that individuals (and by implication independent organizations) may spend as much as they wish to express their own views and advance their own candidacies. The result was a skyrocketing of political campaign spending and an even greater dependence on big money sources of campaign funds than before the passage of the act.

Source: Excerpted from *A Brief History of Money in Politics,* Center for Responsive Politics, Washington, D.C., 1999.

But large individual donations, donations by interest group PACs, and soft money donations by large corporations and unions, are the most important sources of campaign dollars. These are the real "fat cats," many of whom individually contribute more than $1 million *in every national election!* (Tables 4.4 and 4.5, pp. 74 and 75, list the largest contributors to 1996 presidential election and 1998 midterm congressional elections.) Union contributions are heavily weighted toward Democrats, as are the contributions of lawyers, law firms, and the Association of Trial Lawyers. Businesses and business associations tend to split their contributions between the parties, but Republicans usually get the largest share.

Table 4.4 Presidential Election: Twenty-five Largest Contributors, 1996

Rank	Contributor	Total Contributions	Percentage to Democrats	Percentage to Republicans
1.	Philip Morris	$4,208,505	21	79
2.	American Federation of State, County, and Municipal Employees	4,017,553	99	1
3.	Association of Trial Lawyers of America	3,513,588	85	15
4.	National Education Association	3,283,140	96	4
5.	Teamsters Union	3,164,297	96	4
6.	Laborers' Union	3,076,378	93	7
7.	United Auto Workers	3,023,288	99	1
8.	United Food and Commercial Workers Union	2,926,845	99	1
9.	International Brotherhood of Electrical Workers	2,820,528	98	2
10.	American Medical Association	2,794,894	23	77
11.	Communications Workers of America	2,745,264	100	0
12.	AT&T	2,715,101	41	59
13.	Machinists/Aerospace Workers Union	2,565,493	100	0
14.	National Association of Realtors	2,558,358	34	66
15.	Joseph E. Seagram and Sons	2,555,836	67	33
16.	American Federation of Teachers	2,423,088	99	1
17.	National Auto Dealers Association	2,421,575	19	81
18.	R.J.R. Nabisco	2,300,336	20	80
19.	United Parcel Service	2,176,700	35	65
20.	AFL-CIO	2,165,224	98	2
21.	National Association of Letter Carriers	2,151,219	89	11
22.	Federal Express Corp.	2,113,200	46	54
23.	Ernst & Young	1,977,130	51	49
24.	Carpenters Union	1,888,472	46	54
25.	American Institute of Certified Public Accountants	1,853,000	34	66

Source: Center for Responsive Politics from Federal Election Commission data.

Corporations are the principal source of soft money—contributions made to parties rather than to candidates. Corporations may make soft money contributions directly from their treasuries, as may unions, and there is no limit on the size of these contributions. Soft money is the fastest growing source of campaign cash. Efforts to persuade Congress to impose limits on soft money contributions have consistently failed. Lists of the biggest soft money donors in national elections (see table 4.6, p. 76) suggest why: corporate elites dominate these lists.

Table 4.5   Congressional Elections: Twenty-five Largest Contributors, 1998

Rank	Contributor	Total Contributions	Percentage to Democrats	Percentage to Republicans
1.	Philip Morris	$2,596,260	23	77
2.	International Brotherhood of Electrical Workers	2,327,414	98	2
3.	Association of Trial Lawyers of America	2,313,836	86	14
4.	American Federation of State, County, and Municipal Employees	2,097,164	97	3
5.	AT&T	1,772,585	41	59
6.	Teamsters Union	1,731,250	94	6
7.	National Education Association	1,681,314	91	9
8.	National Association of Realtors	1,651,104	40	60
9.	National Association of Home Builders	1,632,240	32	68
10.	Travelers Group	1,631,316	44	56
11.	United Food and Commercial Workers Union	1,587,621	97	3
12.	United Parcel Service	1,578,181	22	78
13.	American Medical Association	1,558,917	33	67
14.	Communications Workers of America	1,514,748	99	1
15.	Amway	1,469,291	0	100
16.	United Auto Workers	1,469,165	99	1
17.	National Association of Letter Carriers	1,463,821	82	18
18.	Bell Atlantic	1,458,277	34	66
19.	National Auto Dealers Association	1,445,905	33	67
20.	BellSouth	1,375,028	45	55
21.	Laborers' Union	1,372,474	91	9
22.	Marine Engineers Union	1,369,585	48	52
23.	Machinists/Aerospace Workers Union	1,356,100	99	1
24.	Boeing	1,349,008	37	63
25.	Lockheed Martin	1,327,386	36	64

Source: Center for Responsive Politics from Federal Election Commission data.

WHAT MONEY BUYS IN POLICYMAKING

What does money buy in the policymaking process? Political campaign contributions are made by moneyed elites with the confidence that the selected candidates are smart enough to know what issues concern the contributors and how to vote in order to keep the contributions coming in the future. A candidate's ability to raise campaign funds is central to the leadership selection process. And assuring contributors of one's understanding and sympathy for their policy posi-

Table 4.6   Soft Money: Twenty-five Largest Contributors, Congressional Elections, 1998

Rank	Contributor	Industry	Total	To Dems	To Repubs
1.	Philip Morris	Tobacco	$1,779,845	$292,823	$1,487,022
2.	Amway	Retail Sales	1,312,500	0	1,312,500
3.	AT&T	Telephone Utilities	844,743	280,240	564,503
4.	American Financial Group	Insurance	735,000	175,000	560,000
5.	R.J.R. Nabisco	Tobacco	701,422	132,572	568,850
6.	Bell Atlantic	Telephone Utilities	683,169	180,300	502,869
7.	Blue Cross/Blue Shield	Insurance	671,950	109,375	562,575
8.	Freddie Mac	Real Estate	625,000	125,000	500,000
9.	Walt Disney Co.	TV/Movies/Music	596,778	294,503	302,275
10.	Travelers Group	Insurance	587,829	169,000	418,829
11.	Buttenwieser & Associates	Education	570,000	570,000	0
12.	Communications Workers of America	Industrial Unions	561,250	561,250	0
13.	BellSouth	Telephone Utilities	542,606	263,027	279,579
14.	Chevron	Oil & Gas	531,260	166,300	364,860
15.	Loral Spacecom	Telecommunications Services & Equipment	526,000	526,000	0
16.	MCI Telecommunications	Telephone Utilities	519,090	218,565	300,525
17.	Pfizer Inc.	Pharmaceuticals/ Health Products	516,550	80,000	436,550
18.	Atlantic Richfield	Oil & Gas	510,456	170,500	339,956
19.	Enron	Oil & Gas	505,500	77,000	428,500
20.	Tobacco Institute	Tobacco	499,700	130,200	369,500
21.	Boeing	Air Transport	475,350	190,800	284,550
22.	Slim-Fast Foods/ Thompson Medical	Food Processing & Sales	450,000	410,000	40,000
23.	Joseph E. Seagram & Sons	Beer, Wine & Liquor	437,675	204,689	232,986
24.	Bristol-Myers Squibb	Pharmaceuticals/ Health Products	434,975	100,300	334,675
25.	Waste Management Inc.	Waste Management	420,525	102,500	318,025

Source: Center for Responsive Politics from Federal Election Commission data.

tions is central to campaign fund-raising. In short, money is the medium of exchange in leadership selection and thus in policymaking.

Campaign contributions are rarely made on a direct quid pro quo basis—direct dollar payments in exchange for sponsoring a bill in Congress or voting for or against a bill in committee or on the floor. Such direct trade-offs risk exposure as bribery and may be prosecuted under law. (It is unlawful to offer to give anything of value in exchange for the performance of a governmental duty.) Bribery, where it occurs, is probably limited to very narrow and specific policy actions—payments to intervene in a particular case before an administrative agency; payments to insert a very specific break in a tax law or a specific exemption in a trade bill; payments to obtain a specific contract with the government. Bribery on major issues is very unlikely; there is simply too much publicity and too much risk of exposure.[2]

Throughout the policymaking process, big campaign contributors expect to be able to call or visit and present their views directly to the officeholders they supported. At the presidential level, major contributors look forward to meeting with the president or at least with high-level White House staff or cabinet members. At the congressional level, major contributors usually expect to meet directly with representatives and senators they have supported. Members of Congress frequently boast of responding to letters, calls, or visits by any constituent. But big contributors anticipate "face time" with the political leaders they helped to put in office.

Some large contributors, especially those that do business with government agencies, also assume members of Congress who they have supported will intervene on their behalf with officials in the bureaucracy. At a minimum, contributors count on their elected representatives to cut red tape, ensure fairness, expedite action on their cases. But many contributors also expect elected officials to intervene and pressure government agencies for favorable decisions.

Generally, the support of policy positions favored by contributors poses no real problems for elected officeholders. Many contributors have very specific policy concerns—concerns that can be addressed by specific, technical changes in the language of laws. Masses are unlikely to even be aware of these kinds of policy actions. Occasionally, however, elected officials confront salient issues— issues that their voting constituents know and care about. When the wishes of major contributors conflict with opinion polls showing the clear preferences of voters, elected officials confront a dilemma.

More often than not, such a dilemma is resolved in favor of the contributor's position. Politicians know that the memory of voters is short, but the memory of contributors is more lasting. The further away in time the next election is, the more likely it is that the dilemma will be resolved in the contributor's favor (see feature: "Tobacco Legislation Goes Up in Smoke").

Yet another way that politicians may resolve this dilemma is to go to their contributors with opinion polls in hand and beg their indulgence. Perhaps contributors can be convinced that some compromises are necessary, that some form of unfavored legislation must be passed. Perhaps it can be watered down to a point where it only symbolically addresses mass concerns without adversely affecting the contributor's interests. Perhaps it can be vaguely worded so that administrative agencies can later be pressured to interpret it favorably with regard to the contributor's interests. Perhaps it can be deliberately worded in a fashion

FEATURE: TOBACCO LEGISLATION GOES UP IN SMOKE

Cigarette smoking is the leading preventable cause of death in the United States. The federal government's efforts to reduce smoking long centered on educating the public to the health dangers involved. In 1964 the U.S. surgeon general first reported (as most people suspected already) that smoking was related to cancer, heart disease, and emphysema. In 1965 Congress required health warnings on every pack of cigarettes sold. In 1970 Congress banned cigarette advertising from radio and television. Over time the percentage of the adult population that smokes has fallen from more than 50 percent in 1965 to about 25 percent today.

As smoking declined, antismoking forces gained political strength in both Washington, D.C., and the states. Various bans on smoking were enacted for domestic air travel, public buildings, areas of restaurants, and so on. But Congress failed to act directly on the national health care costs incurred by smoking.

Traditionally, tobacco companies were very successful in defending themselves against product liability suits. It was difficult for individual smokers to prove in court that their particular illness (cancer, emphysema, heart disease) was produced directly from their smoking. Moreover, the tobacco companies argued that smokers understood the health dangers of smoking and therefore assumed the risk themselves. Indeed, the companies often pointed to the government-imposed warning labels on each pack of cigarettes.

But in 1994 Mississippi and Florida filed civil lawsuits against the major tobacco companies, demanding reimbursement for their states' share of Medicaid costs incurred through smoking-related diseases. In pretrial negotiations with the states, which extended through 1997, the tobacco companies, notably Philip Morris, R.J. Reynolds, and Brown and Williamson, offered a nationwide settlement package. In exchange for dismissing the state cases and limiting the size of damage awards individuals could receive in smoking-related cases, the tobacco companies agreed to total payments of more than $368 billion to the states and to a national fund for children's health. The companies also agreed to end billboard and sports advertising and to take other actions designed to reduce teen smoking over the years. Florida Attorney General Bob Butterworth boasted, "The Marlboro Man will be riding into the sunset on Joe Camel."[a]

Tobacco sales constitute "interstate commerce," however, and Congress was obliged to approve the settlement reached between the states and the tobacco companies. The states begged Congress to give quick approval to the settlement, but Congress huffed and puffed for over a year. Antismoking groups, including the powerful health insurance industry as well as consumer and public interest organizations, added tough amendments to the settlement. The powerful Association of Trial Lawyers opposed reducing the liability of tobacco companies in the hopes that big damage awards and lawyer fees could be won in future cases. The total costs of the congressional version of the settlement to the tobacco companies rose to an estimated $516 billion.

The predictable result was that the tobacco industry turned against the congressional version of the settlement. It mounted a nationwide advertising campaign, at a cost of more than $40 million, that portrayed the congressional proposal as a "tax increase" and the removal of liability limits as a "money grab" by "greedy lawyers." The effect of the campaign was to sway public opinion sufficiently to allow big tobacco's supporters in Congress to vote against the bill without fear of voter retribution. Finally, in June 1998, the U.S. Senate, on a series of procedural votes, killed the tobacco bill. Subsequently, the tobacco companies settled the suits brought by the states for an estimated $200 billion, far less than the original $368 billion agreed to a year earlier.

How did the tobacco companies succeed in preventing Congress from adopting a national tobacco policy?

Big tobacco corporations are a major source of campaign contributions. Indeed, Philip Morris regularly appears at the top of listings of "fat cat" contributors. In recent years this company has been the single largest political donor in the nation. The heaviest beneficiary has been U.S. Senator Jesse Helms, the tobacco industry's number one spokesman in the capital. Some other southern senators receiving heavy support from big tobacco are Mitch McConnell (R-Ky.), Ernest Hollings (D-S.C.), Fred Thompson (R-Tenn.), Jim Bunning (R-Ky.), and Charles Robb (D-Va.).

On the Senate votes that killed the tobacco bill, there is a close correlation between voting for the preferences of big tobacco and the amount of campaign contributions received from the tobacco PACs. The public interest organization Public Citizen claims that senators supporting big tobacco received more than seven times as much campaign money as those opposing big tobacco.[b] Public Citizen also claims that big tobacco spent more than $40 million in direct lobbying expenditures to pressure Congress to kill the amended bill. (See chapter 5 for a discussion of elite involvement in the interest group process.) Nearly 300 lobbyists were employed by big tobacco in 1997 and 1998—one lobbyist for every three members of Congress. Among the powerhouse lobbying firms employed by big tobacco

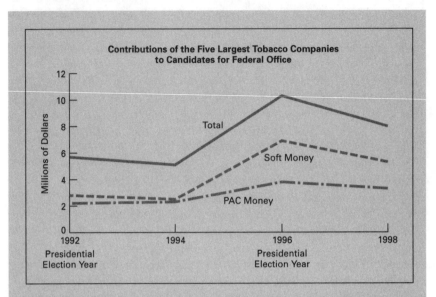

Figure 4A   Big Tobacco Money

was Verner, Liipfert, Bernhard, McPherson & Hand—the firm that employs former Democratic Senate Leader George Mitchell as well as former Republican Senate Leader Bob Dole.

The conclusion was described quite succinctly, albeit somewhat tautologically, by Congresswoman Deborah Price (R-Ohio): "I think the tobacco bill fell apart primarily because you could not find enough votes for it."[c]

a. *Newsweek*, 30 June 1997. See also Thomas R. Dye, *Politics in Florida* (Upper Saddle River, N.J.: Prentice Hall, 1998).
b. Public Citizen, "Blowing Smoke," press release, 17 September 1998.
c. *Congressional Quarterly Weekly Report*, 14 November 1998, 3110.

that will encourage successful court challenge. Indeed, skill in politics is often defined as the ability to successfully resolve conflicts between the preferences of elites and the opinions of the masses.

FINANCING THE PARTIES

Overall, America's elites divide their political contributions fairly evenly between the parties. There are, however, nuances of differences in the sources of financial support for the Democratic and Republican Parties.

The Democratic Party relies heavily on contributions from labor unions. Arguably, union leaders are not a significant component of the nation's elite. They do not control billions of dollars of assets as do leaders of industrial corporations, banks, insurance companies, investment firms, and media conglomerates. They do play a significant role, however, in the leadership selection process, channeling many millions of dollars from their members to favored Democratic candidates. Very little union money goes to the GOP. Public employee unions—notably the American Federation of State, County, and Municipal Employees; the National Education Association; as well as private sector unions, notably the Teamsters, Electrical Workers, Communications Workers, and Auto Workers—are regularly listed among the largest Democratic Party "fat cats" (see table 4.4, p. 74).

Most industries tilt their contributions toward the GOP. Many big corporations, however, choose to fund incumbents regardless of party. The result is that the real estate, health care, insurance, banking, telephone, and pharmaceutical industries usually give at least 30 to 40 percent of their contributions to Democrats (see table 4.7). Tobacco and the oil and gas industries are heavily Republi-

Table 4.7 Campaign Contributions to the Parties by Elite Sector

		TO REPUBLICANS	
Rank	Industry/Interest Group	Total to Republicans	Percentage to Republicans
1.	Insurance	$21,712,512	70
2.	Real Estate	21,085,043	56
3.	Securities and Investment	19,361,441	52
4.	Health Professionals	18,478,331	59
5.	Oil and Gas	16,903,919	77
6.	Lawyers/Law Firms	16,358,121	28
7.	Miscellaneous Manufacturing and Distributing	13,226,047	73
8.	Commercial Banks	11,120,760	65
9.	Leadership PACs	9,369,241	61
10.	Telephone Utilities	9,004,752	61
11.	Automotive	8,568,675	74
12.	Pharmaceuticals/Health Products	8,434,139	65
13.	Air Transport	7,950,536	66
14.	General Contractors	7,912,478	68
15.	Retail Sales	7,865,065	68
16.	Miscellaneous Finance	7,166,203	59
17.	Electric Utilities	7,127,923	66
18.	Food Processing and Sales	7,065,668	71
19.	Business Services	6,910,990	46
20.	Tobacco	6,884,896	80

continued

Table 4.7 (continued)

| | | TO DEMOCRATS | |
| | | Total to | Percentage to |
Rank	Industry/Interest Group	Democrats	Democrats
1.	Lawyers/Law Firms	$42,811,975	72
2.	Securities and Investment	17,220,389	47
3.	Real Estate	16,511,933	44
4.	Public-sector Unions	15,656,730	91
5.	Industrial Unions	13,319,119	96
6.	Health Professionals	12,838,220	41
7.	TV/Movies/Music	10,111,221	61
8.	Transportation Unions	10,045,513	83
9.	Insurance	9,488,744	30
10.	Building Trade Unions	8,582,496	92
11.	Miscellaneous Unions	8,228,114	96
12.	Business Services	8,078,975	54
13.	Commercial Banks	5,865,613	34
14.	Telephone Utilities	5,787,149	39
15.	Education	5,548,854	80
16.	Lobbyists	5,334,013	51
17.	Oil & Gas	5,024,408	23
18.	Miscellaneous Finance	4,782,860	39
19.	Miscellaneous Manufacturing and Distributing	4,679,347	26
20.	Pharmaceuticals/Health Products	4,590,378	35

Source: Center for Responsive Politics from Federal Election Commission data.

Note: Includes PAC soft and individual contributions of more than $200 to federal candidates and parties, for the 1998 congressional elections.

can, although they fund a few influential Democratic Congress members from North Carolina (tobacco) and Texas, Oklahoma, and Louisiana (oil and gas). The Democrats can count on Hollywood—the motion picture and television industries—to help fill their campaign chests.

The Wall Street securities and investment firms divide their contributions evenly between the parties. Among the heaviest of these contributors are Goldman Sachs, Merrill Lynch, Paine Webber, Bear Sterns, Morgan Stanley Dean Witter, Salomon Brothers, and Lazard Freres. Collectively, these firms ranked near the top of both parties' sources of financial support.

Lawyers and law firms are the largest source of campaign money for the Democratic Party. The lawyers' most active interest group—the Association of Trial Lawyers—is a cash cow for the Democrats. But individual Washington lobbying and law firms—for example, Cassidy & Associates, Verner Liipfert, Patton Boggs—must be careful in allocating funds to influential Congress members of both parties. The role of "The Lawyers and Influence Peddlers" is explored in chapter 5.

THE UNLIKELY PROSPECTS FOR REFORM

It is unlikely that the current leadership selection process, with its heavy reliance on moneyed elites and their resulting influence in policymaking, will ever be changed in any significant way.

Most Americans are aware of the power of money in politics. National opinion polls regularly report such responses as the following:

Elected officials in Washington are mostly influenced by what is in the best interests of the country. OR, Elected officials in Washington are mostly influenced by the pressure they receive on issues from major campaign contributors.

	Percentage
Best interests of country	19
Pressure from contributors	77
Neither/Other (vol.)	2
No opinion	2

Source: Gallup/CNN/*USA Today* poll, 3–5 October 1997, as reported in *The Polling Report,* 13 October 1997.

Most elected officeholders, including members of Congress, are themselves frustrated by the constant necessity of raising huge amounts of campaign money. Begging for money is not really a welcome activity. It involves time-consuming personal visits and phone calls to wealthy interests. It requires arranging and attending countless fund-raising dinners and parties. It necessitates constant attention to the calls and requests of lobbyists with ties to big money PACs. Often more of a legislator's time and energy is spent on fund-raising than on either campaigning or legislating. If the decision to end reliance on wealthy contributors were left wholly to its members, Congress would likely do so.

Virtually everyone in Washington gives rhetorical support to campaign finance reform. But hardly anyone can agree on specific reform proposals. Each proposal raises political and sometimes even constitutional issues that obstruct its acceptance.

Proposals to *outlaw PACs* and all contributions by corporations and unions raised constitutional questions about their right to express their preferences and participate in the electoral process. The Supreme Court might strike down a congressional attempt to abolish PACs as a violation of the First Amendment.

Moreover, if PAC money were eliminated, individual contributions would become the only game in town, a situation that would favor Republicans over Democrats.

Proposals to *ban soft money* contributions to political parties directly threaten the power of big money donors. U.S. Senator John McCain led an effort in 1999 to ban soft money; he later made the issue the key to his bid for the Republican presidential nomination. Despite strong popular support for the measure, Senate beneficiaries of big soft money contributions managed to defeat it on procedural votes; few senators wanted to go on record as voting directly in favor of soft money. And it might be noted that soft money gives the parties what little direct influence they have over members of Congress. Cutting off party funding would further weaken the party system.

Proposals to *curtail independent spending and "issue ads"* are likely to be declared an unconstitutional infringement on First Amendment protected free speech.

Proposals to *fund congressional elections publicly* in exchange for agreement by the candidates to place limits on their campaign spending raise a variety of political issues. Public funds currently are available to presidential candidates, yet this has not succeeded in reducing their reliance on big money contributors. Moreover, equal spending by congressional incumbents and their challengers would grant a strong advantage to incumbents, who already have name recognition and years of constituent contracts and services working on their behalf. Indeed, critics charge that public funding with spending limits is really an "incumbent protection" scheme. Finally, most taxpayers are offended by the very idea of politicians using tax dollars to run for public office. Indeed, most taxpayers refuse even to allocate $3 of their taxes to presidential campaigns.

It is doubtful that any reform can ever be devised and approved that will eliminate the influence of big money in the nation's leadership selection process.

CHAPTER 5

The Interest Group Process

Q: Would you say that government is pretty much run by a few big interests looking out for themselves or that it is run for the benefit of all people?
A. A few big interests looking out for themselves—80%
   For the benefit of all—18%
                                        —GALLUP NATIONAL OPINION POLL

INTEREST GROUP ACTIVITY dominates policymaking in Washington. The influence of organized interest groups permeates lawmaking in Congress, rulemaking in federal executive agencies, and, increasingly, decision making in federal courts. And the nation's most powerful interest groups are sponsored and financed by the same corporations, banks, insurance companies, investment houses, law firms, media conglomerates, professional and trade associations, and civic organizations that constitute the nation's institutional elite.

TOP-DOWN REPRESENTATION

Washington is awash in special interest organizations, lawyers and law firms, lobbyists, and influence peddlers. An estimated 15,000 people are officially designated as lobbyists—twenty-five for every member of Congress! Political life in the nation's capital is a frenetic blur of "lobbying," "fund-raising," "opening doors," "mobilizing the grass roots," "building coalitions," "litigating," "rubbing elbows," and "schmoozing." Lobbyists in Washington represent a broad array of interests (see table 5.1, p. 86). But clearly economic organizations dominate interest group politics. Roughly three-quarters of all the lobbyists in Washington represent corporations or business, trade, and professional organizations, or are lawyers from firms representing these interests.

Elite institutions sponsor and finance most of the organized interest group activity in Washington (see figure 5.1, p. 86). Corporate and business interests are represented, first of all, by large inclusive organizations such as the U.S. Chamber of Commerce; the National Association of Manufacturers; and the Business Roundtable, representing the chief executive officers of the nation's largest corporations.

Table 5.1 Types of Lobbyists

Type	Number
Business, trade, and professional organization officers (approximately 2,200 organizations)	5,000
Representatives of individual corporations	1,500
Representatives of special causes	2,500
Lawyers registered as lobbyists	3,000
Public and governmental relations	2,500
Political action committee officers	200
Think tank officers	150

Source: Washington Representatives, 1995 (Washington, D.C.: Columbia Books, 1995).

In addition, specific business interests are also represented by thousands of trade associations, which can closely monitor the interests of their specialized memberships. Among the most powerful of these associations are the American Bankers Association, the American Gas Association, the American Iron and Steel Association, the American Petroleum Institute, the National Association of Broadcasters,

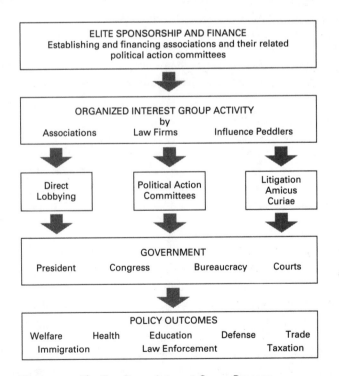

Figure 5.1   The Top-Down Interest Group Process

and the Motion Picture Association of America. Closely allied with the business and trade associations are the professional associations. The American Trial Lawyers Association, the American Bar Association, and the American Medical Association are three of the most influential professional associations in Washington.

Unquestionably, a wide range of other types of organized interest groups are also active in the nation's capital.[1] Although union membership has fallen significantly in recent years, the American Federation of Labor–Congress of Industrial Organizations (AFL-CIO), a federation of more than one hundred separate unions, remains an active player in Washington politics. Many of the larger unions—including the American Federation of State, County, and Municipal Employees (AFSCME); the National Education Association (NEA); the Teamsters; the United Auto Workers; the United Steel Workers; and the United Postal Workers—also exercise considerable clout. These labor organizations are among the largest campaign contributors and they also provide many direct campaign services to their favored candidates (registration, get-out-the-vote drives, information, and endorsements).

Many *noneconomic* organizations lobby in Washington. Few of them have any strong ties to the nation's elite. Instead, many of them have been organized by interest group entrepreneurs—people who create organizations and market membership in them to the masses.[2] These organizations are financed primarily by a combination of membership dues and business activities, such as insurance tie-ins, magazine advertising revenues, credit card sales, travel industry kickbacks, and commercial royalty revenues for endorsing products and services. Thus, for example, the American Association of Retired Persons (AARP), the nation's single largest organized interest group, with 34 million members, is financed by member dues and business activities. For an $8 dollar annual fee, members are offered a variety of services, including discounted rates on insurance, mail-order drugs, hotels, rental cars, and so on. The AARP lobbies in Washington primarily on behalf of expanded Social Security and Medicare benefits.

Interest group representation is not only undertaken by associations, but also by lawyers and law firms, and by independent lobbying firms and influence peddlers. These lawyers and "fixers" in Washington are employed primarily by elite corporations, banks, insurance companies, media companies, and investment houses.

Interest groups influence government policy in a variety of ways. It is possible to categorize efforts to influence government policy as follows:

1. Direct lobbying, including testifying at committee hearings, contacting government offices directly, presenting research results, and assisting in the writing of legislation

2. Campaign contributions made through political action committees (PACs)

3. Interpersonal contacts, including travel, recreation, entertainment, and general "schmoozing," as well as the "revolving door" exchange of personnel between government offices and the industries and organizations representing them

4. Litigation designed to force changes in policies through the court system, wherein interest groups and their lawyers bring class-action suits on behalf of their clients or file *amicus curiae* (friend of the court) arguments in cases in which they are interested

5. Grassroots mobilization efforts to influence Congress and the White House by encouraging letters, calls, and visits by individual constituents and campaign contributors

LOBBYING: WHO IS REALLY REPRESENTED IN WASHINGTON

Direct lobbying expenses provide a good indicator of who is really represented in Washington. While a great many interests maintain organizations in the nation's capital and exercise some influence from time to time, some interests spend a great deal more money than others in pursuit of influence over policy.

Washington's influence industry is a billion-dollar business. Each year lobbyists spend more than $1.25 *billion* dollars trying to influence policy—more than $2 million dollars for each member of Congress! As a result of the Lobbying Disclosure Act of 1995, it is now possible to observe how much money actually does change hands each year in efforts to influence federal policies.

At the industry group level, pharmaceutical and health product manufacturers spend the most on lobbying. This industry's policy priorities include oversight of the activities of the Food and Drug Administration (FDA). The insurance industry ranks second in direct lobbying expenditures, followed by telephone utilities, the oil and gas industry, and electric utilities (see table 5.2). Of the top twenty-five groups spending money on lobbying, only three might be considered noneconomic, nonelite groups. These include governments and public employee unions, educational groups including the National Education Association, and the miscellaneous grouping of single-issue organizations (e.g., AARP, National Rifle Association, Christian Coalition).

Many individual corporations and organizations spend millions of dollars each year in direct lobbying activities. Indeed, at least 200 organizations regularly spend more than $1 million each year in lobbying, and at least fifty organizations spend $5 million or more. The American Medical Association and the tobacco giant Philip Morris are regularly found at the top of the list of big spenders in Washington. Other corporations and organizations that spend more than $10 million dollars each year on lobbying are Bell Atlantic, the U.S.

Table 5.2   Washington's Largest Lobbying Spenders

BY INDUSTRY GROUP

Rank	Industry Group	Direct Lobbying Expenditures, 1997–98
1.	Pharmaceuticals/Health Products	$74,622,930
2.	Insurance	65,904,036
3.	Telephone Utilities	62,142,784
4.	Oil and Gas	61,988,028
5.	Electric Utilities	54,305,778
6.	Health Professionals	43,243,423
7.	Automotive	39,386,094
8.	Tobacco	38,240,340
9.	Business Associations	37,868,943
10.	Miscellaneous Manufacturing and Distributing	37,775,955
11.	Miscellaneous Issues	37,349,551
12.	Air Transport	33,973,401
13.	Securities and Investment	31,058,287
14.	Government Agencies/Civil Servants	30,901,810
15.	Chemical and Related Manufacturing	29,975,745
16.	Commercial Banks	29,912,224
17.	Defense Aerospace	28,345,200
18.	TV/Movies/Music	27,638,640
19.	Education	26,019,335
20.	Computer Equipment and Services	25,474,314
21.	Real Estate	23,267,239
22.	Hospitals/Nursing Homes	22,933,170
23.	Railroads	18,018,527
24.	Telecommunications Services and Equipment	17,129,476
25.	Health Services	12,299,382

BY CORPORATION/ORGANIZATION

Rank	Corporation/Organization	Direct Lobbying Expenditures, 1997–98
1.	American Medical Association	$17,280,000
2.	Philip Morris	15,800,000
3.	Bell Atlantic	15,672,840
4.	U.S. Chamber of Commerce	14,240,000
5.	General Motors	10,600,000
6.	Boeing	10,020,000
7.	Edison Electric Institute	10,020,000
8.	Pfizer Inc.	10,000,000
9.	American Automobile Manufacturers Association	9,916,000

continued

Table 5.2 *(continued)*

Rank	Industry Group	Direct Lobbying Expenditures, 1997–98
10.	Business Roundtable	9,480,000
11.	Citicorp	9,040,000
12.	Blue Cross/Blue Shield	8,761,936
13.	Christian Coalition	7,980,000
14.	American Hospital Association	7,880,000
15.	AT&T	7,800,000
16.	National Committee to Preserve Social Security	7,660,000
17.	Ford Motor	7,343,000
18.	General Electric	7,220,000
19.	Ameritech Corp.	6,800,000
20.	Sprint Corp.	6,740,000
21.	Atlantic Richfield	6,660,000
22.	United Technologies Corp.	6,403,000
23.	National Association of Realtors	6,320,000
24.	Pharmaceutical Research and Manufacturers of America	6,320,000
25.	SBC Communications	6,220,000

Source: Center for Responsive Politics, from Federal Election Commission data.

Chamber of Commerce, General Motors, Boeing, Edison Electric Institute, and the drug giant Pfizer.

It is important to note that direct lobbying expenditures provide only one indicator of an industry's or corporation's clout in Washington. Effective lobbying also requires backup by campaign contributions and in-kind services, election endorsements, and grassroots political support. For example, a survey of Washington insiders conducted by *Fortune* in 1997 ranked the AARP, the American Israel Public Affairs Committee, and the AFL-CIO as the three most powerful lobbies in Congress.[3] Indeed, only about one-half of the magazine's designated "Power Twenty-Five" were industry lobbies; others included the National Rifle Association, the Christian Coalition, the National Right to Life Committee, independent unions (NEA, AFSCME, Teamsters), and veterans' groups.

LAWYERS, LOBBYISTS, AND INFLUENCE PEDDLERS

Thousands of lawyers and lobbyists peddle influence in Washington. But as in all sectors of institutional life in America, an elite few dominate the influence-peddling business.

FEATURE: THE BUSINESS ROUNDTABLE AS SUPERLOBBY

"There are very few members of Congress who will not meet with the president of a Business Roundtable corporation." The Business Roundtable is not only an elite policy planning in coordinating organization (see chapter 3), it is also a direct lobbying organization—indeed, a superlobby. Why does it deserve the title *superlobby?* As one congressional staff member explained: "If a corporation sends its Washington representative to our office, he's probably going to be shunted over to a legislative assistant. But the chairman of the board is going to see the Senator."[a]

The power of the Business Roundtable in policy formulation is augmented by its lobbying power in Washington. The Business Roundtable and the U.S. Chamber of Commerce each spend more than $10 million per year in *direct* lobbying expenditures. More importantly, the power of the Roundtable in Washington also derives from the funds member corporations pour into campaign chests of Congress members (see table). Most of

Business Roundtable Congressional Campaign Contributions, 1998

Organization Name	Total Amount Contributed	Percentage to Republicans	Percentage to Democrats
Philip Morris	$3,006,636	83	17
R.J.R. Nabisco	1,352,931	85	15
AT&T	984,524	56	44
MCI Telecommunications	934,514	36	64
Federal Express	773,525	49	51
Anheuser-Busch	736,057	46	54
Time Warner	726,250	45	55
Chevron	702,306	75	25
NYNEX Corp.	651,602	63	37
Textron Inc.	648,000	58	42
Eli Lilly & Co.	627,825	70	30
Energy Corp.	580,975	49	51
WMX Technologies, Inc.	551,200	66	34
Bank of America	546,798	65	35
Bristol-Myers Squibb	542,400	79	21
Coca-Cola	534,640	67	33
Travelers Group	524,844	62	38
General Motors	501,775	85	15

Source: Center for Responsive Politics from Federal Election Commission data.

the money given by the Roundtable in recent elections has gone to Republicans. But when Democrats controlled Congress, most Democratic incumbents could count on major contributions from Roundtable corporations.

As an interest group, the Business Roundtable wins most but not all of its legislative battles in Washington. The Roundtable lost a lengthy battle over mandated family leaves in 1993 when a Democratic-controlled Congress sent the Family Leave Act to President Bill Clinton to sign as his first major legislative victory. Even more recently, in Republican-controlled Congresses, the Roundtable has been thwarted in its efforts to reform the nation's product liability laws. Its principal opponent in this struggle has been the American Association of Trial Lawyers, itself a major source of campaign financing together with individual law firms. (And, of course, lawyers are the largest single occupational group in Congress itself.) So even with all of its resources, the Business Roundtable does not win all its battles.

The chairman of the Business Roundtable, Robert N. Burt, CEO of the FMC Corporation, said in assuming his chairmanship: "My charge is to ensure that the Roundtable continues to play a major role in setting the course for America on key public policy issues, from trade to health care, education to the environment."[b]

a. Quotations from *Time*, 13 April 1981, 77.
b. Business Roundtable, press release, 4 November 1999.

Heavy-Hitting Lobbyists

More than 100 lobbying firms in Washington earn at least $1 million "representing" heavyweight clients.[4] The top lobbying firms in Washington, ranked by income from lobbying, are shown in table 5.3. The three firms at the top of the list—Cassidy & Associates, Verner Liipfert, and Patton Boggs—regularly contend for the coveted reputation as "the most powerful firm in Washington." All three have more than 100 clients; Patton Boggs leads in the number of clients. But Verner Liipfert boasts of having two former Senate majority leaders—Democrat George Mitchell and Republican Bob Dole—in its employ.

In addition to spending money *directly* on lobbying efforts, the top firms advise their clients on where to send their campaign contributions, and they make their own contributions to members of Congress as well. As table 5.3 suggests, most top Washington firms split their campaign contributions fairly evenly. A few, however, appear to favor Republicans or Democrats. (Barbour, Griffith, and Rogers, for example, is exclusively a Republican firm; its senior partner, Haley Barbour, was formerly the Republican National Chairman.)

The most heavily lobbied policy issues are those dealing with taxation and the internal revenue code, followed by budget and appropriations issues. The

Table 5.3   Top Washington Lobbying Firms, 1998

Rank	Lobbying Organization	Receipts	Total Contributions	Percentage to Democrats	Percentage to Republicans
1.	Cassidy & Associates	$19,890,000	$369,155	63	37
2.	Verner, Liipfert et al.	18,775,000	746,677	58	42
3.	Patton Boggs LLP	14,390,000	208,281	74	26
4.	Akin, Gump et al.	11,800,000	774,173	52	48
5.	Preston, Gates et al.	10,150,000	292,466	44	55
6.	Barbour, Griffith, & Rogers	7,410,000	93,651	0	100
7.	Washington Counsel	7,251,000	63,885	46	54
8.	Williams & Jensen	7,060,000	386,930	40	60
9.	Baker, Donelson et al.	6,820,000	31,895	23	77
10.	Hogan & Hartson	6,546,111	270,485	51	49
11.	Pricewaterhouse Coopers	6,500,000	1,652,090	34	66
12.	Van Scoyoc Associates	6,480,000	114,167	39	61
13.	Timmons & Co.	5,940,000	139,124	50	50
14.	Podesta.com	5,360,000	75,954	82	18
15.	Alcalde & Fay	4,720,000	26,099	79	21
16.	Arnold & Porter	4,660,000	156,303	63	37
17.	Dutko Group	4,632,031	65,228	72	28
18.	Black, Kelly et al.	4,625,000	99,132	33	67
19.	Capitol Associates	4,350,000	60,850	61	39
20.	Meyer, Brown, & Platt	4,260,000	121,565	66	34
21.	Boland & Madigan Inc.	4,200,000	40,030	1	99
22.	Griffin, Johnson et al.	4,180,000	38,403	99	1
23.	McDermott, Will, & Emery	4,109,473	242,750	44	56
24.	Arter & Hadden	4,100,000	141,955	24	76
25.	Wexler Group	4,080,000	167,963	48	52

Source: Center for Responsive Politics.

tax code and appropriations bills are the most likely vehicles for special privileges, treatments, exemptions, favors, and boondoggles.

Professional Go-Betweens

Nearly a half-century ago in his classic book *The Power Elite,* sociologist C. Wright Mills described the role played by the nation's top lawyers and law firms as "professional go-betweens . . . who act to unify the power elite."[5] Go-betweens help to make the top-down policy formulation process function effectively. They are active at all institutional levels—communicating, negotiating, and mediating between corporations, banks, and wealth-holders; foundations and think tanks; and the president, Congress, administrative agencies, and courts. They facilitate the transfer of information among institutional leaders—both substantive information about policy problems and political information about who is likely to support or oppose various solutions. We have labeled them as "go-betweens," but they are often referred to as "superlawyers," "insiders," "expediters," and "fixers."

Superlawyers

Superlawyer go-betweens are most often found among the senior partners of the nation's most prestigious New York and Washington law firms (see table 5.4). The names of these firms do not always identify the senior partners. Firms often retain the names of deceased founders, and most large firms have so many senior partners (often as many as twenty, thirty, or forty) that it is impossible to put all of their names in the title of the firm. In addition, of course, these firms often employ hundreds of lawyers who can only aspire to partnership after many years of service.

The senior partners of the nation's top law firms generally feel an obligation to public service. They believe that the nation's policymaking process requires their knowledge and skills in order to function effectively. The superlawyers do not run for public office; instead, they expect to be appointed to high government posts. For example, an exceptional number of them have served as secretary of state: Warren Christopher (Clinton), Cyrus Vance (Carter), William P. Rogers (Nixon), John Foster Dulles (Eisenhower), Dean Acheson (Truman). Yet many other superlawyers have shunned official government posts, and instead opted to play a go-between role "behind the scenes."

PAC POWER

The real key to successful lobbying by any interest group is its record of campaign contributions. Contributions virtually ensure access to government decision makers. It is highly unlikely that any member of Congress will fail to meet with

---

Table 5.4   The Superlawyer Firms

Arnold & Porter

Covington & Burling

Dewey, Ballantine, Vinson, & Elkins

Wilmer, Cutler, & Pickering

Avent, Fox et al.

Davis, Polk, & Wardwell

Milbank, Tweed et al.

Sullivan & Cromwell

Calinolander, Wickersham, & Taft

Wilkie, Farr, & Gallager

Midge, Rose et al.

representatives of groups that helped to fund his or her election. And top White House staff and Cabinet officials, if not the president, are almost always prepared to meet with interests that have made significant contributions to the presidential campaign. Contributions do not guarantee a favorable decision, but they can be counted on to guarantee a hearing.

Political action committees solicit and receive contributions from members of organizations—corporations, unions, professional and trade associations, as well as ideological, environmental, and issue-oriented groups—and then distribute these funds to political candidates. The first PACs were created by labor unions to circumvent federal laws preventing the direct use of members' dues for political campaigns. Corporations, like labor unions, also had been prohibited from using corporate funds for political campaigns, but prior to the 1970s corporate PACs were relatively rare. It was the passage of the Federal Election Campaign Act of 1974, with its $1,000 limitation on individual contributions to campaigns, that encouraged the rapid growth of PACs by corporations, businesses, professions, trades, and later ideological and issue-oriented groups. During the 1980s a tide of PACs washed over Washington (see table 5.5).

Interest group PACs are now a major source of campaign financing, especially for members of Congress. Overall, about 30 percent of all congressional campaign contributions originate from PACs. PACs provide about 35 percent of the total dollar contributions of winning House members and about 20 percent of contributions of winning Senate members. But because PAC contributions come in larger lumps than individual contributions, PACs attract a great deal of attention from members of Congress. Indeed, many officers of PACs complain about constant harassment by members of Congress—requests to buy tickets to their dinners, cocktail parties, commemorative events, and so on.

PACs are regulated by the Federal Election Commission, which requires them to register their finances and political contributions periodically. A registered PAC that has received contributions from more than fifty people and has

Table 5.5   The Growth of PACs

	1974	1980	1988	1998
Corporate	89	1,206	1,816	1,836
Labor	201	297	354	358
Trade and professional	318	576	786	896
Ideological issue	—	374	1,115	1,259
All other	—	98	197	179
Total number of PACs	608	2,551	4,268	4,528
Total PAC campaign contributions (in millions)	N.A.	$88	$159	$220

Source: Federal Election Commission, 1998.

contributed to at least five campaigns is eligible to contribute $5,000 to any candidate per election and $15,000 to a party's national committee.

PAC contributions are heavily weighted toward incumbents running for reelection. Usually two-thirds of all PAC contributions go to incumbents (see table 5.6); this is true for corporate as well as union and other PACs. All PACs try to get the maximum return on their investments, winning access and influence with as many lawmakers as possible in Washington. They receive no return on their investment if the recipient of their contribution loses at the polls. And PACs are well aware that more than 90 percent of incumbent Congress members seeking reelection win. When Democrats controlled the House of Representatives, most PAC money went to Democrats. When Republicans captured control of the House after the 1994 midterm congressional elections, the weight of PAC contributions shifted to the Republicans.

The really big money PACs are about evenly divided between business and union sponsorship (see table 5.7). Union PACs account for twenty-three of the top fifty PAC contributors, with the Teamsters, government workers, auto workers, and teachers among the top five.

THE CASH CONSTITUENTS OF CONGRESS

Inside the Washington beltway, the interest group process—the activities of corporations and associations, PACs, law firms, lobbyists, and influence peddlers—is well understood. It is seldom talked about by Congress members back home or on the campaign trail, although it is occasionally attacked by their challengers. For

Table 5.6   The Distribution of PAC Money in Congress

| | PERCENTAGE OF PAC CONTRIBUTIONS | | | |
	1997–98	1995–96	1993–94	1989–90
ALL CANDIDATES				
Incumbents	65	67	72	74
Challengers	12	15	10	12
Open Seats	13	18	18	14
SENATE				
Democrats	16	35	50	57
Republicans	18	65	50	43
HOUSE				
Democrats	34	50	67	67
Republicans	32	50	33	33

Source: Federal Election Commission, 1998.

Table 5.7   Fifty Largest PAC Contributors, Congressional Elections, 1998[a]

Rank	Contributor	PAC Total	Percentage to Democrats	Percentage to Republicans
1.	Teamsters Union	$2,647,165	95.8	4.0
2.	American Federation of State, County, and Municipal Employees[b]	2,512,821	98.0	1.6
3.	United Auto Workers[b]	2,475,819	99.2	0.4
4.	American Medical Association[b]	2,442,576	20.1	79.7
5.	National Education Association[b]	2,356,006	98.8	0.8
6.	National Auto Dealers Association	2,346,925	18.2	81.7
7.	Association of Trial Lawyers of America	2,341,938	89.1	10.4
8.	Laborers Union[b]	2,172,450	91.2	8.4
9.	International Brotherhood of Electrical Workers[b]	2,171,262	97.6	2.1
10.	National Association of Realtors	2,099,683	31.2	68.7
11.	United Food and Commercial Workers Union	2,030,795	98.4	1.1
12.	Machinists/Aerospace Workers Union[b]	2,021,175	99.1	0.4
13.	United Parcel Service	1,791,147	35.3	64.7
14.	National Association of Letter Carriers[b]	1,723,228	87.5	11.9
15.	American Institute of CPAs	1,690,925	32.0	67.7
16.	American Federation of Teachers[b]	1,619,635	98.4	1.3
17.	Marine Engineers Union[b]	1,591,365	48.1	51.9
18.	Carpenters Union[b]	1,571,466	94.6	4.9
19.	National Rifle Association[b]	1,560,871	16.6	83.4
20.	United Steelworkers	1,524,650	100.0	0.0
21.	American Bankers Association[b]	1,510,328	29.4	70.3
22.	National Association of Home Builders[b]	1,475,174	17.7	82.3
23.	National Association of Life Underwriters	1,426,750	31.0	69.0
24.	AFL-CIO[b]	1,399,056	97.4	2.3
25.	Communications Workers of America[b]	1,390,686	99.4	0.1
26.	National Beer Wholesalers Association	1,324,992	16.6	83.4
27.	AT&T[b]	1,311,232	36.1	63.9
28.	American Dental Association[b]	1,309,120	34.3	65.7
29.	United Transportation Union[b]	1,266,500	83.4	15.7
30.	National Association of Retired Federal Employees	1,245,350	83.3	16.5
31.	Plumbers/Pipefitters Unions	1,149,735	95.0	4.6
32.	Lockheed Martin[b]	1,126,750	27.3	72.7
33.	National Committee for an Effective Congress	1,113,475	99.3	0.2

continued

Table 5.7 *(continued)*

Rank	Contributor	PAC Total	Percentage to Democrats	Percentage to Republicans
34.	National Federation of Independent Business	1,074,543	6.4	93.2
35.	Sheet Metal Workers Union[b]	1,065,500	96.8	2.7
36.	Federal Express	948,000	29.3	70.6
37.	Americans for Free International Trade	936,800	11.4	88.6
38.	National Restaurant Association[b]	933,634	12.5	87.5
39.	Operating Engineers Union[b]	908,290	89.7	10.0
40.	American Hospital Association[b]	893,026	48.5	51.4
41.	Ernst & Young[b]	886,365	50.2	49.8
42.	Philip Morris[b]	883,619	26.7	73.2
43.	Air Line Pilots Association[b]	880,000	77.8	22.2
44.	BellSouth[b]	870,867	33.4	66.5
45.	Ironworkers Union[b]	849,115	94.6	5.0
46.	Campaign America	829,971	0.5	99.4
47.	Service Employees International Union	820,950	99.6	0.3
48.	Associated General Contractors[b]	805,050	6.0	94.0
49.	Union Pacific Corp.[b]	800,357	12.7	87.3
50.	American Nurses Association	791,508	88.9	10.4

Source: Center for Responsive Politics, from Federal Election Commission data.

a. Does not include soft money contributions to political parties
b. Contributions came from more than one affiliate or subsidiary

the most part, these activities are conducted out of the public limelight—in Capitol offices and hallways, in committee rooms, around conference tables, and in the plush offices of lawyers and lobbyists on K Street. Lobbyists have their greatest influence on the *details* of public policy. A few lines in a 1,000-page tax or appropriations bill can mean hundreds of millions of dollars to specific corporations, firms, and individuals. (See feature: "There's Big Money in Banking," pp. 100–102.)

The mass public may not be aware of the specific activities of corporations, lawyers, lobbyists, and PACs in Washington, but the public generally believes that these actors have "too much power and influence" (see figure 5.2), especially in comparison with public opinion. Voters may be wrong in thinking that all members of Congress are crooks, but they are right to worry that Congress members pay more attention to their cash constituents in Washington than to their voting constituents back home.

How much power do interest groups and their PACs really have over congressional legislation? Do PAC contributions merely gain "access" to Congress members? Or do PAC contributions directly sway votes on key legislative issues?

The Harris Poll. 11–15 February 1999. N=1,007 adults nationwide:
*"Do you think . . . have/has too much or too little power and
influence on Washington?"*

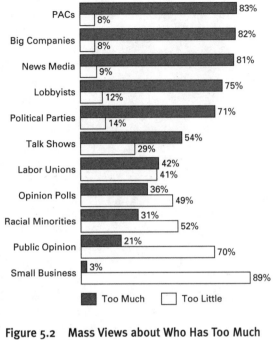

Figure 5.2   Mass Views about Who Has Too Much
              Influence in Washington

Source: *Polling Report,* 1 March 1999, 7.

It is difficult to develop evidence of a direct link between PAC contributions
and specific roll-call votes of Congress members.[6] First, the leadership selection
process ensures that members generally hold views compatible with those of the
elites that sponsor interest group PACs. Thus, the views of members may coin-
cide with the positions of interest group PACs independently of direct PAC
contributions.

Second, the key details of legislation are worked out in committee rooms and
staff meetings. The most important effects of interest group lobbying and PAC
contributions may not be found on roll-call votes but rather on the various earlier
stages of legislative process, including the behind-the-scenes negotiation over
specific provisions, the drafting of amendments, and the markup of bills in
committees and subcommittees (see chapter 9).

Finally, it is rare that one finds a roll-call vote which presents a clear conflict
between the preferences of a Congress member's home constituents and the posi-

FEATURE: THERE'S BIG MONEY IN BANKING

There's big money in banking—not only in the financial industry itself but also in Washington when Congress considers legislation affecting banking and finance. Indeed, in recent years "banking reform" may have generated more political money than any single piece of congressional legislation in history. The Financial Services Modernization Act of 1999 is not the type of legislation that very many people outside of elite circles know about. Yet it will have very important long-term effects on mass consumers in America as well as on the structure of the nation's elite system.

During the Great Depression of the 1930s, banks, investment firms, and insurance companies came under intense criticism as contributors to the nation's economic instability. The result, early in the administration of President Franklin D. Roosevelt, was the Glass-Steagall law, officially the Banking Act of 1933, that forced a separation between the banking and securities industries. The act was intended to protect bank depositors from having their funds intermingled with those of stock market speculators or speculated with by banks themselves.

In recent decades, megamergers of giant financial groups successfully circumvented the act. (For example, Citibank first merged with the Salomon Brothers and Smith Barney investment firms, and then later with Travelers Insurance, to create the megacorporation Citigroup. Former Secretary of the Treasury Robert Rubin was named cochairman of Citigroup following the merger.) But these key sectors of America's national elite still resented the Glass-Steagall law and began to call for its outright repeal in the 1980s. Progress was slowed, however, due to squabbling between banks, investment firms, and insurance companies over specific provisions of what they referred to as "banking reform." But by 1999, a general settlement had been reached; the Glass-Steagall Act was repealed and the "financial services" industry was freed of many bothersome government restrictions. The Financial Services Modernization Act is designed to allow the creation of giant financial supermarkets that will provide one-stop services to consumers—commercial banking; mortgage loans; life, health, home, and auto insurance; corporate and bond stock underwriting; and mutual fund, stock, and bond brokerage services.

"Banking reform" was accompanied by one of the largest spending sprees in American politics. Between 1993 and 1998, banks, investment firms, and insurance companies took in nearly $250 million in soft money, PAC, and individual campaign contributions. More than $100 million was spent by these industries in the 1998 midterm congressional election alone. Both Democratic and Republican candidates prospered, but Republicans, having control of both houses of Congress in 1994, received the bulk of this largesse. About 40 percent of these contributions went to members of the committees that dealt directly with the content of the repeal bill—the House Banking and Senate Banking Committees. And, not surprisingly, the

Big Money in Banking

Total Campaign Contributions (Soft Money, PAC, and Individual) by Financial Electors,[a]
1998 Midterm Congressional Election

Company	Total
INVESTMENT FIRMS	
Goldman, Sachs & Co.	$1,912,866
Citigroup[b]	1,051,608
Merrill Lynch	1,025,141
Morgan Stanley Dean Witter	889,294
Bear Stearns	832,181
Paine Webber	715,927
M.A. Berman Co.	660,850
Chicago Mercantile Exchange	648,300
J.W. Childs Associates	572,250
Investment Co. Institute	564,937
Total: Securities	51,660,995
INSURANCE COMPANIES	
American Financial Group	1,472,645
Blue Cross/Blue Shield	1,415,690
National Association of Life Underwriters	1,355,500
Citigroup[b]	1,085,708
AFLAC	1,000,470
American Council of Life Insurance	841,005
American International Group	768,465
Independent Insurance Agents of America	661,514
Cigna	615,960
Alfa Mutual Insurance	532,000
Total: Insurance	41,711,427
BANKS	
BankAmerica	1,732,650
American Bankers Association	1,466,786
Bank One	1,259,588

J.P. Morgan & Co.	659,344
Chase Manhattan	633,061
America's Community Bankers	590,176
Citigroup[b]	471,430
Independent Bankers Association	469,804
First Union	429,352
Wells Fargo	387,503
Total: Banking	20,875,266

Source: Center for Responsive Politics, based on Federal Election Commission data

a. Top ten campaign contributors, 1998, in each sector.
b. Based on FEC data. Totals include contributions from subsidiaries.

top individual recipient (of nearly $2 million) was U.S. Senator Phil Gramm (R-Tex.), chairman of the Senate Banking Committee.

The top corporate contributors from the banking, securities, and insurance industries in the 1998 congressional elections represent the core of America's financial elite (see table). In addition to their campaign contributions, these industries incurred more than $250 million in direct lobbying expenses over the two years prior to the passage of "banking reform."[a]

a. Center for Responsive Politics, 1999, according to figures reported by lobbyists under the terms of the 1995 Lobby Registration Act.

tion of the member's contributing PACs. Voting constituents seldom know about specific legislation or have a clear-cut position on a bill voted on by the House or Senate. Moreover, the legislative process is deliberately designed to adjust and compromise bills prior to final passage in order to avoid obvious conflicts between Congress members' cash constituents and their voting constituents.

CHAPTER 6

The Opinion Making Process

The power of the press in America is a primordial one. It sets the agenda of public discussion; and this sweeping political power is unrestrained by any law. It determines what people will talk about and think about—an authority that in other nations is reserved for tyrants, priests, parties, and mandarins.

—THEODORE WHITE

THE NATION'S MEDIA elite occupy a unique position in the top-down policy-making process. The leadership of the nation's most influential media institutions—the *Wall Street Journal,* the *New York Times, Washington Post–Newsweek, Time, U.S.A. Today,* Capital Cities–ABC, Disney–CBS, General Electric–NBC, Fox Broadcasting, Turner Communications–CNN—are themselves an important component of the national elite. Indeed, today leadership of the mass media has established itself as equal in power to the nation's corporate and governmental leadership.

But the media also play another role in the policymaking process—that of communicating elite views to government decision makers and the masses of Americans. The media carry elite messages directly to government officials, most of whom begin their day by scanning the *Washington Post,* or the *New York Times,* or the *Wall Street Journal,* or browsing the Internet news sites, and watching television network morning news. For most of Washington, the news stories and opinion columns that appear each morning set the agenda for conversation for the rest of the day. And the media also determine what the *masses* of Americans will know about, think about, and talk about. Most Americans report that they get most of their news from television and that television news is more believable than any other source of information.

In short, the media in America are both an important component of the nation's top elite *and* an instrument in the policymaking process for communicating elite views to both government officials and the general public.

TOP-DOWN OPINION MAKING

Media corporations are seldom ranked among the nation's largest industrial or financial institutions. Media moguls occupy their seats in America's top leadership echelon not because of their control of economic resources but rather because of their control of information. Their power arises from their ability to decide what is "news," to interpret the news, to socialize mass audiences to the political culture, to provide a means for mass persuasion, and, above all, to set the agenda for political discussion. Perhaps in no other society does the media exercise so much power independently of government and other social and economic institutions.

Elite opinion making flows downward through the media to both government and the mass public (see figure 6.1). Elites depend on media to define societal "problems," to create "issues," and to prepare government and the mass public for the introduction of "solutions" in the form of new or revised public policies. The media are the principal means of elite communication with both government officials and the general public.

Media are themselves large corporations, and they are strongly influenced by the advertising and public relations activities of other corporations. Advertising is a *$200 billion* business in the United States. Television receives the largest single portion of this largesse, closely followed by newspapers. Corporations use these

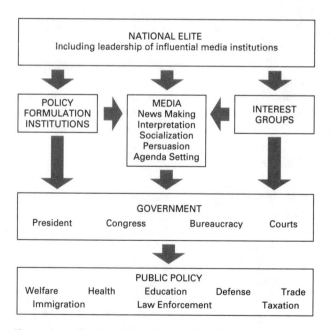

Figure 6.1   The Top-Down Opinion Making Process

advertising dollars not only to promote sales of their product but also to convey the message that they are good citizens sensitive to the environment, concerned with consumer safety, and devoted to providing more and better jobs, goods, and services to America. Corporate public relations also operate primarily through the mass media. Corporations and independent public relations firms employ thousands of former journalists, TV reporters, and other media people in their direct efforts to shape public opinion.

The institutions of policy formulation—the foundations, "think tanks," and policy planning organizations—communicate their policy proposals both directly to government and indirectly to government and the mass public through the media. A great deal of the work in think tanks consists of writing press releases, preparing "op-ed" pieces (opinion and editorial essays), responding to reporters' inquiries, giving television interviews, and arranging press conferences for the release of policy proposals. Likewise, interest groups spend much of their time and energy in media relations—preparing "press kits" that set forth their arguments and supporting information, arranging "media events" designed to attract media coverage of their concerns, and scrambling to "make the evening news," if only for a few precious seconds. The media act as "gatekeepers" in all of this activity, deciding whose messages will be passed on to government and the public and whose will not.

The power of the media in policymaking lies in creating issues, publicizing them, dramatizing them, turning them into "crises," getting people to talk about them, and ultimately forcing government officials to do something about them. Media inattention creates nondecisions. It allows conditions in society that might otherwise be labeled as problems to be ignored by government: "TV is the Great Legitimator. TV confers reality. Nothing happens in America, practically everyone seems to agree, until it happens on television."[1]

The media directly cue government officials about topics to which they must turn their attention. Politicians are forced to respond to reporters' questions about specific topics. They cannot respond by saying, "That's not really important." They may try to avoid specific commentary on particularly controversial issues, but by doing so they risk the worst of all fates in politics—being ignored.

THE ELITE MEDIA

Media power—the power to decide what most Americans will see, hear, and read about their world—rests largely with a small number of private corporations (see feature, "The Media Empires," pp. 106–7). Despite the multiplication of channels of communication in recent years, media power remains concentrated in the leading television networks (ABC, CBS, NBC, FOX, CNN), the nation's influential national newspapers *(Washington Post, New York Times, Wall Street Journal,* and *USA Today),* and the broad-circulation news magazines *(Time, Newsweek, U.S. News & World Report).*

FEATURE: THE MEDIA EMPIRES

Media megamergers in recent years have created corporate empires that spread across multiple media—television, film, print, music, and the Internet. These global conglomerates combine television broadcasting and cable programming, movie production and distribution, magazine and book publication, music recording, sports and recreation, and now Internet access and e-commerce. The seven multinational corporations listed below dominate world media and cultural markets.

General Electric, Sony, and Seagram were originally industrial corporations; they bought into the media world. General Electric (GE appliances, aircraft engines, industrial products) is the largest of these corporations, but its ownership of media brings in only about 5 percent of its corporate revenue. Sony (a Japanese electronics multinational) receives only 30 percent of its corporate revenue from media operations. Seagram (a Canadian distillery) now receives more revenue from media enterprises than from its whiskey sales. Walt Disney, Viacom, and NewsCorp (Fox) are true media conglomerates.

The largest empire of all, AOL-Time Warner Inc., spreads itself beyond television, cable, motion pictures, magazines, books, sports, and entertainment, into cyberspace. Time Warner was already a merged corporate conglomerate, the largest true media empire, *before* its merger with the nation's largest Internet provider, America Online. Time, Inc., originally a news magazine publisher *(Time, People, Sports Illustrated, Fortune,* etc.) had merged with Warner Communications, originally a motion picture production company, in 1989. Then Time Warner merged with Ted Turner–owned CNN, Turner Broadcasting, and the Atlanta Braves, in 1996. One of the biggest mergers in American corporate history was announced in early 2000: the two giants of their respective industries—Time Warner, the media conglomerate, and America Online, with 22 million Internet subscribers—combined to form a new colossus. The combined stock market value of AOL and Time Warner is greater than that of any other corporation in America.

The Media Empires

1. AOL-Time Warner
   Television: HBO, TNT, TBS, CNN, CNNSI, CNNFN, Cinemax, Time Warner
   Cable
   Motion Pictures: Warner Brothers, New Line Cinema, Castle Rock
   Magazines: Time, People, Sports Illustrated, Fortune, plus twenty-eight
   other specialty magazines
   Books: Warner Books, Little, Brown Publishing, Book-of-the-Month Club

Music: Warner Brothers Records, Atlantic Records, Elektra

Sports and Entertainment: Atlanta Braves, Atlanta Hawks, World
    Championship Wrestling

Internet: AOL, Netscape, CompuServe

2. Walt Disney

Television: ABC-TV, plus ten stations; ESPN, ESPN-2, Disney Channel,
    A&E, E!, Lifetime

Motion Pictures: Walt Disney Pictures, Miramax, Touchstone

Music: Walt Disney Records, Mammoth

Sports and Recreation: Disney theme parks in Florida, California,
    France, Japan; cruise line; Anaheim Angels, Mighty Ducks

3. Viacom

Television: CBS, plus thirty-four TV stations; MTV, TNN, Nickelodeon,
    Showtime

Motion Pictures: Paramount Pictures, Spelling, Viacom

Books: Simon & Schuster

Music: Famous Music Publishing

Sports and Recreation: Blockbuster Video, SportsLine, plus five
    Paramount parks

4. NewsCorp (Fox)

Television: Fox Network plus fifteen TV stations; Fox News, Fox Sports,
    Fox Family Channel

Motion Pictures: 20th Century Fox, Searchlight

Books: HarperCollins

Music: Mushroom Records

Sports and Recreation: Los Angeles Dodgers

5. Seagram

Television: USA Network

Motion Pictures: Universal Pictures

Music: MCA, Geffen, Def Jam, Motown

Sports and Recreation: Universal Studios theme parks in California and
    Florida

6. Sony

Television: Game Show Network

Motion Pictures: Columbia Pictures, Sony Pictures, Tri Star

Music: Columbia Records, Epic Records, Nashville Records

Sports and Recreation: Sony Theaters

7. General Electric

Television: NBC Network plus thirteen TV stations; CNBC,
    MSNBC

Television is the most powerful medium of *mass* communication. Television is regularly chosen over other news media by Americans as not only their "most important" source of news, but also as their "most believable" source of news (see figure 6.2). It is true that the national network evening news shows have lost viewership in recent years (down from a combined average of 40 million viewers in 1980 to 28 million today). But viewership of cable CNN and its headline companion HNN is rising, and viewership of local television news has remained strong. Moreover, television news magazines, notably CBS's *60 Minutes* and ABC's *20/20*, are regularly listed among the most popular shows on television. And television tabloids, such as *Hard Copy* and *Inside Edition*, are also gaining viewers.

The most influential New York and Washington newspapers are not so much instruments of mass communication as they are vehicles for *interelite* communication. It is especially important for top government officials to be familiar with both news stories and opinion columns that appear each day in the *Washington Post, New York Times, Wall Street Journal,* and *USA Today*. About 1,800 separate newspapers are published daily throughout the nation and read by approximately 70 percent of the adult population. But many of the news stories and virtually all of the opinion columns dealing with national affairs that appear in local newspapers throughout the country are taken from the national press.

News magazines have a somewhat broader readership than the New York and Washington press. *Time* is the nation's leading weekly news magazine, with a circulation of more than 4 million, followed by *Newsweek* and *U.S. News &*

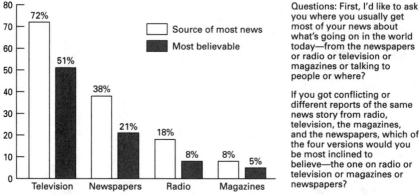

Figure 6.2   Media Influence with the Masses

Note: Percentages (for sources of news) add up to 125 percent due to multiple responses. For trend line on these questions, see Harold W. Stanley and Richard G. Niemi, *Vital Statistics on American Politics, 1997–1998* (Washington: Congressional Quarterly Press, 1998). Between 1962 and 1964, television passed newspapers as a source of most news. Between 1958 and 1960, television passed newspapers as the most believable medium.

World Report. But the masses are more concerned with human interest stories, television and entertainment "news," travel, and tending their gardens—*Modern Maturity, Readers Digest, TV Guide, National Geographic,* and *Better Homes and Gardens* far exceed all news magazines in circulation.

Half of all Americans claim to have read at least one book in the past year. But virtually all of the most-read books are textbooks, self-help books, or popular fiction. Serious, nonfiction books dealing with public affairs are largely limited to elite readership. Nonetheless, a few of these books have been influential in the opinion making process. For example, Michael Harrington's *The Other America* built support for President Lyndon Johnson's Great Society antipoverty programs in the 1960s; Rachel Carson's *Silent Spring* helped to launch the environmental movement; E.S. Savas's *Privatizing the Public Sector* provided a guide for conservative reform of government operations in the 1980s; David Osborne's *Laboratories of Democracy* gave Democratic centrists a handbook for governmental renewal; welfare reform in the 1990s was inspired by Charles Murray's 1984 book *Losing Ground;* the educational voucher movement was spurred by John E. Chubb and Terry M. Moe's *Politics, Markets, and America's Schools;* Allan Bloom's *The Closing of the American Mind* inspired concern about the nation's declining cultural standards; and so on. But again, serious books on public affairs, like the New York and Washington press, can be categorized as *interelite* communication.

In contrast, the motion picture industry strives to maintain and enlarge its mass audiences. About 250 feature films are produced each year and shown in 12,000 local theaters nationwide. Very few contain any social or political messages, although the making of "message movies" is becoming somewhat more fashionable in Hollywood today.

Radio, specifically talk radio, is the only form of mass communication in America today, aside from the Internet, that is truly populist in character. That is to say, talk radio does *not* reflect elite values and interests, but rather the concerns and passions of its mass audiences. The most popular talk radio figures—people such as Rush Limbaugh and G. Gordon Liddy—reflect, if anything, antiestablishment views.

THE MEDIA IN THE OPINION MAKING PROCESS

"He who determines what politics is about runs the country."[2] The media's principal source of power is their ability to set the political agenda for the nation. *Agenda setting* is the power to decide what will be decided. It is power to define society's "problems" and thus create political issues.

The issues receiving the most media attention become the issues that the general public comes to view as most important. It is true that media coverage is more influential in determining what public thinks *about* than it is in determining what the public thinks. Media can create new opinions more easily then they can change existing ones. And the media have more influence over topics and issues beyond the realm of personal experience—topics and issues about which the masses have no prior feelings or experiences. In short, the mass media may not be successful in telling us what to think, but they are stunningly successful in telling us what to think about."[3]

Deciding what will be the news—*news making*—is the daily task of the national press and television networks. The media does not simply mirror reality; it is not a "picture of the world." On the contrary, each day national media must select from millions of events, topics, and people, those that will become the news. Indeed, the national media must screen thousands of reports, miles of videotape, and the many hundreds of commentators and pundits offering opinions, to determine what will be fitted onto the news and editorial pages and squeezed into network news broadcasts. (Allowing for commercials, only twenty minutes of the half-hour network evening news programs can be devoted to news.) Decisions about what will be shown or printed define the news making function.[4]

The media's power extends beyond news making to the *interpretation* of the news. Each news item is a story that must be placed in a context and given meaning. Each major news story begins with a "lead-in," usually a statement about the importance of the news to readers and viewers. The selection of "visuals"—photographs in newspapers and videotapes on television—is crucial to interpretation; people remember pictures better than words. The "voice-over" on television and the caption under the newspaper photo tell us what the visuals mean. Stories without good visuals—without dramatic photos or videotape—are less likely to be selected as news.

Interpretation also occurs in the selection of "sources." The media tend to select sources that express the media's views about the importance and meaning of a news item. Even when the media decide to report on two sides of a controversy, they can tilt the debate by their choice of sources. When the media support a position, spokespersons are selected who are personally appealing, articulate, and attractive. When the media oppose a position, spokespersons for that position are likely to be unattractive, bumbling, or obnoxious.

The power of the media also extends to *socializing* the masses. Socialization extends throughout news reporting, entertainment programming, and product advertising. Most of the political information that people learn comes to them through television—both specific facts and general values. Election coverage, for example, demonstrates "how democracy works." Entertainment programming tries to socialize people in acceptable ways of life—for example, racial tolerance, sexual equality, support for law enforcement—even while dramatizing violence, crime, and corruption. Realistic "docudramas" portray specific political themes from abortion to drug use, child abuse, and AIDS. "Infotainment" shows such as *60 Minutes* and *20/20* attract large audiences, as do the tabloid entertainment news shows. Indeed, the line between news and entertainment is no longer really visible. Finally, advertising shows Americans desirable middle-class standards of living, encouraging people to buy automobiles, beer, and computers.

The media are continually engaged in direct *persuasion*. Most direct persuasion efforts, of course, are made in paid commercial advertising. But newspaper editorials have traditionally been used for direct persuasion. And political commentary on television news and interview programs is often aimed at persuading people to adopt the views expressed. Research indicates that the media are far more successful in agenda setting, and even somewhat more successful in opinion shaping, than they are in persuading people to change their views or behaviors.

The effects of the media on *behavior* are difficult to determine. There have been many studies of the effects of violence and sex portrayed in the media.[5] Although it is difficult to generalize from these studies, the media appear more likely to reinforce behavioral tendencies than to change them. For example, televised violence may trigger violent behavior in children who are already predisposed to such behavior, but televised violence appears to have little behavioral effect on average children. And political advertising in campaigns appears to be more successful in motivating a candidate's supporters to go to the polls and cast their votes, than it is in changing opponents into supporters.

THE POLITICS OF THE MEDIA

The politics of the media is driven principally by their economic interests. The media must capture and hold the largest possible mass audiences. This economic motive creates a strong bias toward sensationalism in news making. To attract viewers and readers, the media must emphasize violence, scandal, corruption, crime, sex, and scares of various sorts. The news must "touch" audiences, arouse emotions, and hold the interest of people with short attention spans. Scare stories—bombings and terrorism, mass killings, drug abuse, AIDS, global warming, and a host of health alarms—make "good" news from the perspective of the media because they attract the attention of the masses. Indeed, crime is the leading topic of television network news; crime stories are twice as frequent as the next leading topic—health scares of various sorts. The sex lives of politicians, once by custom off-limits to the press, are now public "affairs." Corruption in government and greed in business are favorite media themes. The media are biased toward bad news because bad news attracts larger audiences than good news. Indeed, research indicates that bad-news stories on television outnumber good-news stories by ten to one.

Moreover, the professional training and environment of working reporters and editors encourage an activist style of "adversarial journalism." The press sees itself as a "watchdog" of the public trust. Reporters see themselves in noble terms—crusaders for justice, the defenders of the disadvantaged, and enemies of corruption, greed, lawlessness, and evil in high places. Success in watchdog reporting brings professional accolades, including Pulitzer prizes for "investigative reporting." "The watchdog function, once considered remedial and

FEATURE: THE CONFLICTING POLICY VIEWS OF MEDIA AND BUSINESS ELITES

The policy views of the media elite are decidedly liberal and reformist: "Economic and social liberalism prevails, as does a preference for an internationalist foreign policy."[a]

Media elites describe themselves as political liberals, in clear contrast to business elites (see table). And the media's liberalism is reflected in a wide variety of policy views. Unlike business elites, large majorities of media elites believe that government should redistribute income from haves to have-nots. Media elites are much stronger supporters of affirmative action, abortion rights, and homosexual rights than are business elites.

Conflicting Views of Business and Media Elites

	Business Leaders	Press Reporters	Television Producers
IDEOLOGY			
Liberal economic views	13%	54%	75%
Government should redistribute income	23	68	69
Government should guarantee jobs	29	48	45
SOCIAL VIEWS			
Support strong affirmative action	71%	80%	83%
Women should have the right to abortions	80	90	97
Homosexuals should not teach in schools	51	15	15

Source: Robert Licter and Stanley Rothman, "Media and Business Elites," *Public Opinion* (October/November 1981); Linda S. Licter, Robert Licter, and Stanley Rothman, "Hollywood and America," *Public Opinion* (December/January 1983).

Because media elites control the flow information and opinion to masses, liberal policy views receive more public airing than conservative views. As noted, however, the media's liberalism is not necessarily shared by other elites in American society. Moreover, the masses themselves are aware of the liberal bias of the media. Nearly three out of four Americans (74 percent) see "a fair amount" or "a great deal" of bias in news coverage. And of those who see a bias, at least twice as many see a liberal bias (43 percent) as see a conservative bias (19 percent). A large majority (63 percent) complain about "one-sided coverage" in the media, and most believe that the media have "too much influence" (58 percent).[b]

a. Doris A. Graber, *Mass Media and American Politics* (Washington, D.C.: CQ Press, 1980), 49
b. Data on mass opinion from *Media Monitor,* May/June 1997, Center for Media and Public Affairs, Washington, D.C.

subsidiary . . . [is now] paramount: the primary duty of the journalist is to focus attention on problems and deficiencies, failures and threats."[6]

Watchdog reporting also reflects the liberal and reformist politics of the media. Leaders in the news and entertainment industries in America are much more liberal in their views than leaders in business and finance (see feature, "The Conflicting Policy Views of Media and Business Elites"). Liberals in the media believe that spotlighting the negative aspects of American life will lead to social reforms.

But the media's preferences for dramatic and sensational stories, bias toward negativism in American life, and regular exposures of wrongdoing in high places frequently place them at odds with other elites. Corporations, banks, Wall Street investment firms, lawyers and law firms, lobbyists, and influence peddlers all come under regular attack by the media. Even in movies and television entertainment shows, politicians usually are depicted as corrupt and self-seeking, corporate executives as greedy and insensitive, generals as self-serving and bloodthirsty, and even religious leaders as crooked and hypocritical. It is not surprising that this negativism creates considerable tension between media elites and leaders of other institutions in society.

Elites in other sectors of society frequently complain about the adverse societal effects of regular media reporting of violence, crime, corruption, and scandal. Mass distrust of government, feelings of powerlessness, declining voter participation, and a lack of confidence in America's institutional leadership (see table 6.1) have all been attributed to "television malaise."[7]

Table 6.1   Declining Mass Confidence in America's Institutional Leadership

Q: I am going to name some institutions in this country. As far as the people running these institutions are concerned, would you say you have a great deal of confidence, only some confidence, or hardly any confidence at all in them?

Percentage saying "a great deal"

	1973	1983	1993	1998
Big business	29	24	21	11
Banks	32	24	15	16
Medicine	54	52	39	16
Television	19	12	12	15
Newspapers	23	18	11	14
Military	32	29	42	33

Source: Surveys by the National Opinion Research Center, 1973–93, as reported in *American Enterprise,* November/December 1993; and Gallup/CNN/*USA Today,* 1998, as reported in *The Polling Report,* 22 June 1998.

Top-Down Media Effects

In our top-down policymaking model, media influence flows through multiple channels. The media influence government decision making *directly* when politicians in Washington are obliged to respond to reporters' questions, news reports, and editorial opinions. The media influence policymakers *indirectly* by calling public attention to various societal "problems," "issues," and "crises." And finally, the media heavily impact the *leadership selection process* by driving up costs of campaigning and thereby making candidates ever more dependent on moneyed elites.

Directly Influencing Government Officials

The media set the policy agenda by choosing questions to pose directly to government officials. Presidents, press secretaries, cabinet officials, congressional leaders, and their staffs, all confront reporters and TV cameras virtually every day. They must be prepared to give "good head"—snappy sound bites for headlines and television interviews—on whatever topics or issues are raised by the media. They are obliged to be ready to give some response to reporters' questions, whether or not they have ever given any prior thought to the topics. If, as is frequently the case, they do not wish to take a policy position on an issue, they must at least invent a quotable evasion.

Politicians have a love-hate relationship with the media. They need media attention to promote themselves, and they crave media exposure and the name recognition and celebrity status that the media can confer. At the same time, they fear attack by the media; they understand the power of the media to make or break their careers. Politicians cannot respond to reporters' questions with "no comment," "that's not important," or "I don't really have any opinion about that." Reporters' questions actually force politicians to confront issues posed by the media.

Influencing Mass Opinion

While the media generally are successful in telling the mass public what to think about, the media are seldom able to change preexisting values or opinions. Viewers and readers frequently screen out messages and opinions with which they disagree. This "selective perception" leads people to see and hear only what they want to see and hear. So many messages are directed at viewers and readers each day that they cannot possibly process them all. "Information overload" is especially heavy in politics and public affairs. The media tell people more about politics than they really want to know.[8] Selective perception and information overload severely reduce the ability of the media to shape opinion on issues on which the masses have already formed views.

Nonetheless, when mass opinion does change, it changes in the direction favored by the media. Although most people's opinions remain constant over time (opinion at an early time period is the best predictor of opinion at a later time period), opinion *changes* are heavily influenced by the media.[9]

Further Empowering Moneyed Elites

Television has further enhanced the power of moneyed elites by driving up the costs of political campaigning. Candidates are forced to raise ever larger sums of money each election cycle to meet the continually rising costs of television advertising. Long ago, television replaced local party organizations and grassroots neighborhood campaigning as the principal means of communicating with voters. Today most candidates spend more time fund-raising to pay for television ads than they do directly contacting voters.

The costs of campaigning have risen dramatically as candidates have been forced to employ professional media consultants, spend money on polling and focus groups, contract with advertising firms to produce spot commercials, and buy television time to broadcast ads. The first question aspiring candidates confront today—from city hall to county courthouse to state capital to Washington—is how much money they can raise. Unless candidates are personally wealthy, they are obliged to seek financial support from moneyed elites (see chapter 4).

CHAPTER 7

The Policy Legitimation Process

To choose a government is not to choose governmental policies. Whereas the voters largely do determine the players in the game of American politics, they have far less control over the signals players will call, the strategies they will employ, or the final score. The popular will, as represented by a majority of voters, does not determine public policy.

—GERALD M. POMPER

ONLY GOVERNMENTS CAN claim *legitimacy* in the use of force to achieve policy goals. It is true that private individuals and organizations—from muggers, gangs, and crime families, to violent revolutionaries and terrorists—may use force to get what they want, but only governments can claim to use force legitimately—that is, people generally believe that it is rightful for government to use force when necessary to uphold the law. Achieving legitimacy, then, is essential in government policymaking.

Democratic governments have a special claim to legitimacy. These governments allow citizens to participate in the selection of leaders. People who disagree with a law are told to work for its change by speaking out, petitioning, demonstrating, joining interest groups, and participating in political party activity. They are told that they may vote to oust those elected officials who supported the law, or even run for public office themselves. Thus, democratic government imposes a special moral obligation on citizens to obey the law, inasmuch as citizens are granted the opportunity of "working within the system" to change the law.

Elites in a democratic society must work to ensure that their policies are viewed as legitimate by the masses: "Once it has been decided that a certain program is required as a response to a policy problem, that choice must be made a legitimate choice. . . . It is by means of the official process of government that substantive policy decisions are legitimated; that is, the policies have the legitimate authority of the state attached to them by the process."[1]

TOP-DOWN POLICY LEGITIMATION

Legitimacy in the top-down policymaking process is *not* achieved by popular vote. Popular policy initiatives and referenda votes are characteristic of only about half of the *state* governments in the United States. The Founders of our nation made no provision in the U.S. Constitution for national referenda. Indeed, direct popular participation in policymaking was viewed by the Founders as a dangerous threat to individual liberty. As James Madison explained, in classic elite fashion, "the public voice, pronounced by representatives of the people, will be more consonant with the public good than if pronounced by the people themselves."[2]

Rather, policy legitimacy at the national level is achieved by elected leaders—members of Congress and the president acting within constitutional boundaries, functioning within institutional structures, and performing under accepted procedures that reassure the masses that the rules of the game have been followed. Elections, parties, interest groups, and all of the other paraphernalia of democracy provide "symbolic reassurance" to the masses of the legitimacy of the laws. The functions of these democratic processes are primarily to "quiet resentments and doubts about particular political acts, reaffirm belief in the fundamental rationality and democratic character of the system, and thus fix conforming habits of future behavior."[3] Elections function primarily to give legitimacy to government authority, to obligate the masses to abide by policies enacted by government.

In the top-down policymaking model, policies themselves do not originate from the citizenry, nor are they subject to popular approval. The institutional system, not the policies themselves, legitimates policy.

THE LIMITS OF CONSTITUENCY INFLUENCE

Legitimacy does *not* arise out of any congruence between the policy views of "the people" and the laws enacted by Congress. Indeed, considerable evidence indicates a *lack* of congruence between the policy preferences of the American public and current national policies on a number of highly visible issues (see feature: "Public Policy versus Mass Preferences," pp. 118–19). In other words, there is little evidence to support a "bottom-up" view of congressional decision making.

Members of Congress like to think of themselves as independent-minded, public-spirited "trustees," rather then merely message-carrying "delegates" sent to Washington by their districts' voters. The philosophical justification for this notion was offered by the English parliamentarian Edmund Burke more than 200 years ago in a speech to his constituents: "Your representative owes you, not his industry only, but his judgment; and betrays, instead of serving you, if he sacrifices it to your opinion."[4]

But the rationale for Congress members' independence from constituency influence may not be so noble as that implied by Burke. Members know that their constituents are largely unaware of their voting records in Congress. Indeed, only 25 percent of American voters can name both of their U.S. senators and only 29 percent can identify their representative.[5] And even among constituents who know a congressperson's name, very few have any idea what his or her policy positions are on major issues.[6] Only occasionally, on a highly publicized vote, where home state or district feelings are intense, will a member defer to constituents' views over

FEATURE: PUBLIC POLICY VERSUS POPULAR PREFERENCES

Public policy in America varies a great deal from popular preferences. If the bottom-up policy process model (described in chapter 1) actually characterized policymaking in America, we would expect public policy to reflect popular preferences fairly closely. But that is not the case, even on policy issues on which the masses are relatively well-informed and hold strong opinions.

A Comparison of Mass Policy Preferences and Current Public Policy

Suppose that on Election Day this year you could vote on key issues as well as candidates. Please tell me whether you would vote for or against each one of the following propositions. (Twenty-seven items read in random order)

			MASS PREFERENCE		
			Percentage For	Percentage Against	Current Policy
1.	*Balanced budget amendment	Yes	83	14	No
2.	Raising the minimum wage	Yes	83	15	Yes
3.	*English as the official language	Yes	82	16	No
4.	Life sentences for drug dealers	Yes	80	17	Yes
5.	Death penalty for murder	Yes	79	18	Yes
6.	*Congressional term limits amendment	Yes	74	23	No
7.	*Prayer in public schools amendment	Yes	73	25	No
8.	*Reducing all government agencies	Yes	71	23	No
9.	Two-year cutoff for welfare without work	Yes	71	24	Yes
10.	Mandatory job retraining	Yes	69	25	Yes
11.	*Doctor-assisted suicide	Yes	68	29	No
12.	*School choice	Yes	59	37	No
13.	*Teaching creationism in public schools	Yes	58	36	No
14.	*Ban on partial-birth abortions	Yes	57	39	No
15.	Ban on assault rifles	Yes	57	42	Yes
16.	*Five-year freeze on legal immigration	Yes	50	46	No
17.	*Federal flat tax system	Yes	49	39	No
18.	Reducing social spending	No	44	53	No
19.	Reducing defense spending	No	42	54	No
20.	Abortion ban except to save mother's life	No	42	56	No
21.	Reestablishing relations with Cuba	No	40	49	No
22.	*School busing for racial balance	No	34	62	Yes
23.	Legalization of gay marriages	No	28	67	No
24.	Selling off public lands	No	24	70	No
25.	Legalization of marijuana	No	24	73	No

26. Withdrawal of U.S. from United Nations	No	17	77	No
27. *Racial preferences in jobs and school	No	14	83	Yes

Source: Public opinion percentages from *The Gallup Poll Monthly*, May 1996.
Note: An asterisk indicates that policy differs from mass preference.

Popular preferences differ from current government policies on a variety of key issues. The national survey of public opinion on twenty-seven "hot button" issues produced results shown in the table. Mass support or opposition is shown by percentages; current public policy is indicated by a "Yes" or "No." Asterisks placed in front of specific issues indicate those in which current public policy differs from popular preference. Note that *on almost half of the issues polled, public policy differs from mass preference.*

Opinion surveys have regularly reported strong public support for passing a balanced budget constitutional amendment, making English the official language of the United States, placing limits on Congress members' terms of office, allowing prayer in public schools, reducing the size and spending of government agencies, allowing parents to choose public or private schools for their children, prohibiting partial-birth abortions, and adopting a flat-rate income tax. The mass public has consistently opposed racial balancing in public schools and racial preferences in education and employment, yet these policies remain in effect throughout most of the country.

those of the party's leadership. As one congressman put it, "They don't know much about my votes. Most of what they know is what I tell them. They know more of what kind of a guy I am. It comes through in my letters: 'You care about the little guy.' "[7] A long record of "home-style" politics—doing case work for constituents, performing favors, winning pork barrel projects for the district, frequent visits back home to "press the flesh"—can protect members from any opposition that might be generated by their voting records.[8]

Most Americans are aware that they have very little influence in the policy-making process. Only 9 percent of adults believe that politicians represent the American people; more than three-quarters of the general public believe that politicians "belong to a Political Class with its own agenda" (see table 7.1, p. 120). Only one out of three Americans believes that the government reflects the will of the people; almost half say that it does not, while 20 percent are not sure. More than two-thirds of the general public believe that the federal government has become "a special interest group that looks out primarily for its own interests." Moreover, a majority of Americans believe that the government does not pay much attention to what they think in its decision making; and more than two-thirds of the public do not believe that government understands what people think. Finally, it is interesting to note that the American public believes that the nation would be better off if leaders "followed the views of the public more closely."

Table 7.1   Mass Views of Their Own Influence in Policymaking

Q1: Do American politicians represent the American people, or do they belong to a Political Class with its own agenda?

Represent the people	9%
Belong to a Political Class	77
Not sure	14

Q2: Despite its flaws, our political system is a government that accurately reflects the will of the American people.

True	34%
False	47
Not sure	20

Q3: The federal government has become a special-interest group that looks out primarily for its own interests.

True	68%
False	16
Not sure	16

Q4: Would it be a good idea to place limits on the federal government so that federal spending and taxes could not increase faster than inflation and population growth?

Yes	81%
No	8
Not sure	11

Q5: Over the years, how much attention do you feel the government pays to what people think when it decides what to do?

A good deal	7%
Some	36
Not much	54

Q6: In general, do you think people in government understand what people like you think very well, somewhat well, not that well, or not well at all?

Very well	2%
Somewhat well	27
Not that well, or not well at all	68

Q7: If leaders of the nation followed the views of the public more closely, do you think the nation would be better off or worse off than it is today?

Better	81%
Worse	10
Don't know	10

Source: Questions 1–4: Rasmussen Research, 6 April 1998; questions 5–7: Center on Policy Attitudes, 31 January 1999, as reported in *The Polling Report*, 15 February 1999.

CONGRESS AND LEGISLATIVE LEGITIMACY

Congress is designated in the U.S. Constitution as the principal instrument of policy legitimation. Article I describes the national government's powers, for example "to lay and collect Taxes, Duties, Imposts, and Excises," as powers of *Congress*. It is important to note, however, that Congress is not the exclusive repository of policy legitimacy. Courts also bear a heavy responsibility to maintain the legitimacy of governmental authority, and to a somewhat lesser extent, so do administrative bureaucracies. By focusing attention on Congress in the policy legitimation process, we do not mean to detract from the importance of other governmental institutions in maintaining legitimacy.

But Congress currently faces a crisis in legitimacy. National polling evidence indicates that Congress enjoys less popular confidence than most other major institutions in American society. Congress is the least popular branch of the national government (see table 7.2). Most Americans believe that members of Congress "spend more time thinking about their own political futures than they do passing legislation."[9]

Table 7.2   Mass Confidence in Institutions

Q: Now I'm going to read you a list of institutions in American society. Please tell me how much confidence you, yourself, have in each one: a great deal, quite a lot, some, or very little.

Percentage saying "a great deal" or "quite a lot"

The military	64
The church or organized religion	59
The police	58
Small business	56
The presidency	53
Business and industry	40
The U.S. Supreme Court	50
Banks	40
The medical system	40
Public schools	37
Television news	34
Newspapers	33
Big business	30
Organized labor	26
Congress	**28**
The criminal justice system	24

Source: Gallup/CNN/ *USA Today* poll, 1998, as reported in *The Polling Report,* 22 June 1998.

Yet Congress has developed highly institutionalized rules and procedures to help legitimate its actions. Indeed, its rules and procedures have become so elaborate that proposed policy changes are extremely difficult. Very few of the bills introduced in Congress are passed; in a typical two-year session, more than 10,000 bills are introduced, but fewer than 800 (less than 10 percent) are enacted in any form. Congress is accurately perceived among both elites and masses as an obstacle rather than a facilitator of policy change.

The formal process of lawmaking is outlined in figure 7.1. The familiar path, "How a Bill Becomes a Law," is taught in virtually every high school civics and college government class in the nation. But this outline of the formal lawmaking process fails to describe the hopes, fears, and ambitions of the members of Congress; the dominant role of leadership in both the Senate and House of Representatives; the powerful influence of partisanship; the central importance of the institutionalized customs, norms, and traditions of each body; and, above all, the continually pressing need of members of Congress to raise money for their reelection campaigns.[10]

AMBITION, PROFESSIONALISM, AND INCUMBENCY

Few members of Congress are elites themselves. Few can afford to get elected or reelected to Congress using only their own financial resources. Only occasionally does a Kennedy, Danforth, or Heinz decide to pursue a career in Congress. The vast majority of Congress members have climbed the ladder to political success from relative obscurity.

"Political office today flows to those who want it enough to spend time and energy mastering its pursuit. It flows in the direction of ambition—and talent."[11] People who run for and win congressional seats are *not* the wealthiest or most successful business or professional people in their states. Instead, they are the most politically ambitious people—people who are willing to sacrifice time, family, and private life for the celebrity that comes with public office. Their talent is that of political entrepreneurship—the ability to sell oneself to others as a candidate, to raise money from contributions, to organize people to work on one's behalf, and to communicate and publicize oneself through the media.

Today political officeholding is largely professionalized. Citizen-statesmen—people with business or professional careers who serve in public office part-time or for short periods of time—have largely been driven out of political life by career politicians—people who enter politics early in life as a full-time occupation and make it their career.

Ambitious young people start out as interns or staffers with members of Congress, on congressional committees, or in state legislators' or governors' offices, or even as volunteer workers in political campaigns. They find political mentors, learn how to organize campaigns, and most important, learn how and where to contact financial contributors. Within a few years they are ready to

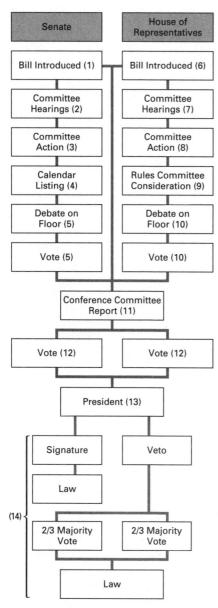

Figure 7.1 How a Bill Becomes a Law

1. **Introduction.** Most bills can be introduced in either house. (In this example, the bill is first introduced in the Senate.) It is given a number and referred to the proper committee.

2. **Hearings.** The committee may hold public hearings on the bill.

3. **Committee action.** The full committee meets in executive (closed) session. It may kill the bill, approve it with or without amendments, or draft a new bill.

4. **Calendar.** If the committee recommends the bill for passage, it is listed on the calendar.

5. **Debate, amendment, vote.** The bill goes to the floor for debate. Amendments may be added. The bill is voted on.

6. **Introduction to the second house.** If the bill passes, it goes to the House of Representatives, where it is referred to the proper committee.

7. **Hearings.** Hearings may be held again.

8. **Committee action.** The committee rejects the bill, prepares a new one, or accepts the bill with or without amendments.

9. **Rules Committee consideration.** If the committee recommends the bill, it is listed on the calendar and sent to the Rules Committee. The Rules Committee can block a bill or clear it for debate before the entire house.

10. **Debate, amendment, vote.** The bill goes before the entire body and is debated and voted upon.

11. **Conference Committee.** If the bill as passed by the second house contains major changes, either house may request a conference committee. The conference—five persons from each house, representing both parties—meets and tries to reconcile its differences.

12. **Vote on conference report.** When committee members reach an agreement, they report back to their respective houses. Their report is either accepted or rejected.

13. **Submission to the president.** If the report is accepted by both houses, the bill is signed by the Speaker of the House and the president of the Senate and is sent to the president of the United States.

14. **Presidential action.** The president may sign or veto the bill within ten days. If the president does not sign and Congress is still in session, the bill automatically becomes law. If Congress adjourns before the ten days have elapsed, it does not become law. (This is called the "pocket veto.") If the president returns the bill with a veto message, it may still become law if passed by a two thirds majority in each house.

run for local office or the state legislature. Over time, running for and holding elective office becomes their career.

The cost of running for Congress today virtually guarantees the dependency of its members on financial elites. Corporations, interest group PACs, and individual "fat cats" become the *real* constituents of Congress members (see chapter

4). Most members of Congress spend hours each day making fund-raising calls from their offices on Capitol Hill. "Making your calls" is a basic responsibility of the job. And a fat campaign chest brings immediate rewards—other members who have confidence in your reelection and staffers who need not fear for their jobs. Many well-heeled incumbents not only amass large campaign chests for their own future use, but also establish their own PACs to give money to other members, adding considerably to their own influence within Congress.

Incumbents seeking reelection almost always win. Indeed, more than 90 percent of House members seeking reelection are successful (see table 7.3). Senate incumbents are only slightly less successful. The advantages of incumbency are many: the name recognition on the ballot that helps direct the choice of poorly informed voters; the ability to use the resources of their congressional office—staff time, travel funds, perks, and privileges—to tend to the needs of their constituents; the franking privilege for mailing newsletters, push polls, and other information to voters; and two years of appearances at various public events, news conferences, and meetings of civic, charitable, and educational organizations in the district.

But the most important advantage of incumbency is the ability to raise money. Smart money backs winners, and smart money knows that incumbents almost always win. Indeed, incumbents usually raise and spend twice as much money as their challengers (see table 7.3).

Does money buy election to Congress? In about 90 percent of all congressional races, the candidate who spends the most money wins. Because so many winning candidates are incumbents, however, the money differential between incumbents and challengers may reflect the expected political outcome rather than shape it. But even in open-seat races, the candidate who spends the most money usually wins.[12]

PARTY AND LEADERSHIP

Congress itself is governed by a top-down, hierarchical leadership system (see figure 7.2, p. 126). Party organizations within the House of Representatives and the Senate are the bases for organizing Congress. The leaders of each house, although nominally elected by the entire chamber, are actually chosen by secret ballot of the members of each party—in the Republican and Democratic conferences (in the House, the Democratic caucus). The majority party in each chamber proceeds to vote unanimously on behalf of its chosen candidates for Speaker of the House and president pro tempore of the Senate; the majority party in each chamber selects the majority leader of the Senate and the majority leader of the House; the minority party selects its own minority leader of the Senate and minority leader of the House. Perhaps more important, *the majority party in each house ensures that it has a majority of the members of every committee, and that the chairman of every committee is a majority party member.*

Table 7.3   Incumbent Advantage

INCUMBENTS RAISE MORE CASH

	House	Senate
Average incumbent	$628,064	$5,015,685
Average challenger	301,289	2,418,075
Average open-seat candidate	638,571	2,970,011

AND INCUMBENTS ALMOST ALWAYS WIN

Year	Percentage of House Incumbents Reelected	Percentage of Senate Incumbents Reelected
1966	90	96
1968	96	83
1970	95	88
1972	93	84
1974	90	92
1976	96	61
1978	95	68
1980	92	59
1982	90	93
1984	96	90
1986	98	75
1988	98	77
1990	97	96
1992	87	86
1994	91	92
1996	94	95
1998	98	91

Source: Federal Election Commission, 1998; *Congressional Quarterly Weekly Report.*

Of course, the parties and their leaders do not choose congressional candidates. Party leaders cannot deny members of Congress nomination by their party or reelection by their home constituents. But party leadership in each house can indeed help or hinder incumbents in the achievement of these goals.

The Speaker of the House serves as both presiding officer of that chamber and leader of the majority party. It is the Speaker who decides who shall be recognized to speak on the floor and whether or not a motion or amendment is relevant to the business at hand. The Speaker decides to which committees new bills will be assigned. The Speaker appoints members of select, special, and conference

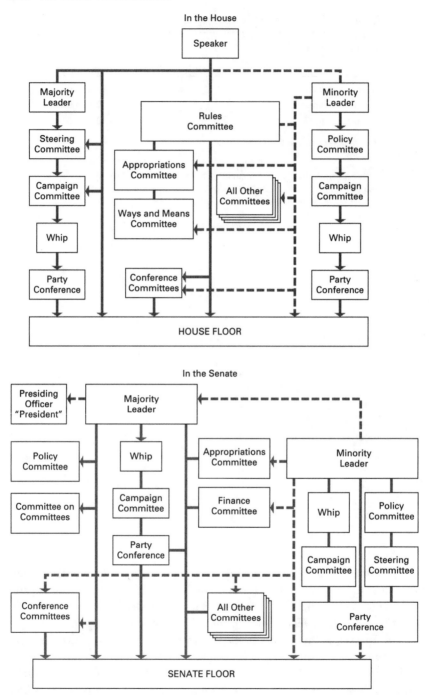

Figure 7.2 Top-Down Leadership

committees and names majority-party members of the important Rules Committee. The Rules Committee, together with the Speaker, decide what bills will actually come to the floor, how long they will be debated, and what amendments, if any, will be allowed. And the Speaker controls both patronage jobs and office space in the Capitol. The majority leader of the House assists the Speaker in these tasks, helping to steer the party's legislative program through the House.

Senate leadership rests with the majority leader. But the majority leader is not as powerful in that body as the Speaker is in the House. With fewer members, the Senate is less hierarchically organized than the House. The Senate has no Rules Committee to limit debate or sidetrack amendments on the floor. Instead, the Senate relies on unanimous consent agreements negotiated between the majority leader and the minority leader to govern floor consideration of a bill. But as the name of the process implies, a single senator can object to a unanimous consent agreement and thus hold up Senate consideration of any bill. Senators do not usually do so, however, because they know that a reputation for obstructionism will endanger their own bills at a later date. Yet the Senate cherishes its tradition of unrestricted floor debate. Any senator, or more likely any group of senators, can attempt to halt passage of a bill by withholding unanimous consent and threatening to continue debate (filibuster) until the leadership is forced to drop the bill to get on with other business. A filibuster can be ended only if sixty or more senators vote for cloture. Effectively this means that a supermajority is required to pass legislation against a determined opposition. And in recent decades neither the Republican nor the Democratic Party has been able to win sixty seats in the Senate.

Another source of leadership power in Congress is the ability to direct campaign money to loyal party members. Both the Republican and Democratic Parties maintain House and Senate campaign committees with their own war chests. These committees provide only a small proportion of total congressional campaign funds, but they can play an important role in a few close electoral battles. And individual leaders in both the House and the Senate maintain "leadership PACs" to assist loyal supporters. In the 1998 midterm election alone, leadership PACs distributed more than $10 million to congressional candidates (see table 7.4, p. 128).

Party loyalty is far stronger among Congress members and other political activists than it is among voters. Party-line votes—roll-call votes in the House and Senate on which a majority of Democrats vote in opposition to a majority of Republicans—occur on more than half of all the roll call votes in Congress. Indeed, party-line votes appear to have risen in recent years, indicating an increase in partisanship in Washington (see figure 7.3, p. 128). Party unity in Congress—the average percentage of support among members of each party for their party's position on party-line votes—is also fairly high. On average, both the Democratic and Republican Parties can expect more than 80 percent of their members to support their party on a party-line vote (see table 7.5, p. 129).

Table 7.4 Congressional Leadership PAC Contributions

SENATE

Al Gore, vice president	$1,192,500
Trent Lott, Republican majority leader	581,998
Don Nichols, Republican majority whip	286,133

HOUSE OF REPRESENTATIVES

Bob Livingston, (former) Speaker	662,380
Newt Gingrich, (former) Speaker	765,500
Dick Armey, Republican majority leader	879,892
Richard Gephardt, Democratic majority leader	365,508
Tom DeLay, Republican majority whip	389,082
Dennis Hastert, Republican Speaker	107,322

TOTALS

Total Amount (all leadership PACs)	10,857,360
Total to Democrats	3,012,304
Total to Republicans	7,841,056

Source: Center for Responsive Politics.

Note: Figures shown are contributions made to other members by congressional leadership PACs in 1998.

Of course, party loyalty and party-line voting in the Congress may not necessarily be a product of top-down leadership discipline in the parties. They may result more from ideological or issue agreement among members of each party than from party organization or leadership. Nonetheless, it is the party leader-

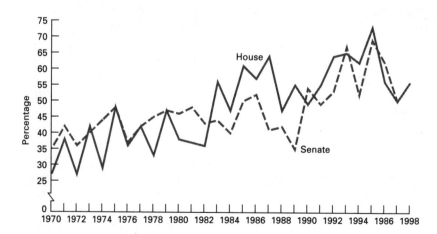

Figure 7.3   The Rise of Partisan Voting in Congress

Table 7.5 Party Unity in Congress

Year	Percentage of Party Support—Democrats	Percentage of Party Support—Republicans
1990		
Senate	82	77
House	86	78
1992		
Senate	82	83
House	86	84
1994		
Senate	84	79
House	83	84
1994		
Senate	84	89
House	80	87
1998		
Senate	87	86
House	82	86

Source: Congressional Quarterly Weekly Report, various years.

Note: Average percentage of times a member voted with majority of party of affiliation in disagreement with the other party's majority.

ship, especially the majority party leadership, that sets the agenda for congressional decision making.

THE COMMITTEE SYSTEM

The committee system with its seniority rules creates another top-down leadership hierarchy in Congress. The standing committees of the House and the Senate (see table 7.6, p. 130) are the gatekeepers of Congress. With rare exceptions, bills are not submitted to a vote by the full membership of the House or the Senate without prior approval of a standing committee. Moreover, committees do not merely sort through the bills assigned to them and approve what they like. Rather, committees—or their subcommittees—amend, rewrite, and write their own bills. Committees are "little legislatures" that jealously guard their own policy jurisdictions.

The chairmen of the most powerful standing committees—notably, in the Senate, the Appropriations, Finance, Judiciary, and Foreign Relations Commit-

Table 7.6   Standing Committees in Congress

SENATE

Agriculture, Nutrition, and Forestry	Governmental Affairs
Appropriations	Indian Affairs
Armed Services	Judiciary
Banking, Housing, and Urban Affairs	Labor and Human Resources
Budget	Rules and Administration
Commerce, Science, and Transportation	Small Business
Energy and Natural Resources	Special Aging
Environment and Public Works	Veterans' Affairs
Finance	Select Ethics
Foreign Relations	Select Intelligence

HOUSE OF REPRESENTATIVES

Agriculture	National Security
Appropriations	Resources
Banking and Financial Services	Rules
Budget	Science
Commerce	Small Business
Education and the Workforce	Standards of Official Conduct
Government Reform and Oversight	Transportation and Infrastructure
House Oversight	Veterans' Affairs
International Relations	Ways and Means
Judiciary	Select Intelligence

tees; and in the House the Rules, Appropriations, Ways and Means, and Judiciary Committees—are powerful figures in Washington. Generally these chairman decide whether or not to hold hearings on bills and they decide the agenda of the full committees. The chairmen appoint the committees' staff members, allocate the committees' often substantial budgets, and, of course, usually receive the largest campaign contributions from the major interests within the committees' jurisdictions. Their committees virtually become "fiefdoms" over which they exercise great power, often independently and occasionally even in conflict with, their House or Senate party leaders. Interest groups, bureaucrats, and the media all must consult the chairmen on all questions relating to their committees in their policy areas. The committee system has become so institutionalized in Congress that an attack on the authority of one committee or committee chairman is likely to be thought of as a threat to all. Members know that if they allow one committee or chairman to be bypassed, they open the door to similar infringements of their own powers and prerogatives. Hence, committees and especially committee chairman support one another's authority over legislation assigned to their respective committees.

Committee chairs are officially designated by the majority party conference. The seniority system, however, governs most selections of committee leadership positions. The seniority system ranks all committee members of each party according to the length of time they have served on the committee. When an opening occurs in a chairmanship, it is filled by the next highest ranking majority party member. In effect this means that leadership in the committee system is vested in those members who have acquired the longest tenure in office. These are usually members elected from noncompetitive congressional districts.

New members of a committee are initially added to the bottom of the ranking of their party in that committee; they climb the seniority ranking by remaining on the committee and accruing years of seniority. New members strive for assignments to the most influential committees. These assignments are handed out by the party leaders in the House and Senate when new members arrive at the Capitol. Nearly every new member seeks a seat on Appropriations, because both the House and Senate Appropriations Committees actually control federal spending. And the House Ways and Means Committee and the Senate Finance Committee (the tax writing committees of each chamber) are also very popular, as are the Judiciary Committees of both houses (civil rights, judicial appointments, etc.). Foreign Relations and Armed Services in the Senate are also considered prestigious committees. But every committee and its chair exercise great power over its own policy area.

The power of the standing committees in Congress is partially diluted by the proliferation of subcommittees. Currently the House has about 150 subcommittees and the Senate about 90 subcommittees. Many of these subcommittees, notably Appropriations subcommittees, have become tiny "subgovernments" within their own specialized policy area. Often it is these subcommittees that form the core of the close knit "policy networks" that dominate policymaking in particular issue areas. These policy networks are frequently referred to as the "iron triangles" of policymaking—subcommittee members and staff, interest group representatives, and executive agency bureaucrats. But all actions by subcommittees must be approved by their full standing committees before going to the full House or Senate chamber for consideration. While standing-committee members generally respect the actions of subcommittees (inasmuch as they also sit on their own subcommittees and expect respect in return), subcommittee work is occasionally discarded by the standing committee, especially when the standing-committee chair disagrees with the subcommittee's views.

Conference committees function very differently from standing committees. A bill must pass both houses of Congress in identical form before it goes to the president for his signature and becomes law. Any differences between a House or Senate bill require that bill to be either resubmitted to one or the other chamber for acceptance, or submitted to a conference committee composed of members of both houses to iron out specific differences. Disagreements between houses are so frequent that more than one-third of all bills, including virtually all important ones, must go to conference committees. When and if a conference committee reaches agreement, the bill, now officially known as the "conference report," must be approved by a full vote of both houses.

Thus, conference committees and their members become powerful actors in the policymaking process at a key point. Conference committees are appointed to consider specific bills; that is to say, conference committees are impermanent. They are appointed by the leadership of each house. They usually come from the two standing committees that handled the bill in each house, and they almost always include the chairs of both committees as well as the ranking minority-party members of those committees. As with the standing committees, a majority of the conference committee members will be from the majority party of their house. Conference committees enjoy great power in shaping the final legislation; they are not obliged to accept either the House or Senate wording of any provision but may in fact write new wording themselves. Both houses must accept or reject conference committee reports as a whole. They cannot amend them; doing so returns the bill to the conference committee and therefore defeats it. Most conference committees are closed and unrecorded; they hold no hearings and listen to no outside testimony. They may even insert provisions in bills that were never voted on by either house. It is little wonder that conference committees are frequently referred to as "the third house" of Congress.

Money and Legitimacy

Corporations, banks, law firms, unions, lobbyists, and fat cat contributors do not hand over billions of dollars to politicians without expecting a return on their investment. Chapters 4 and 5 argue that money is crucial in the candidate selection process and that it buys access to decision makers for the special interests. But admittedly, following the money trail from contribution to *specific* policy enactment is difficult.[13]

Congress members themselves usually concede that money buys access—that contributions play an important and often decisive role in determining who gets to talk with members in their inner offices and plead their case. According to one congressman, "people who contribute get the ear of the member and the ear of the staff. They have the access. Access is power. Access is clout. That's how this thing works."[14]

But members of Congress deny that money "buys" votes, although interestingly these same members often agree that many of their colleagues are not as "principled" as they are. According to one member of Congress, "on the tax side, the appropriations side, the subsidy side, and the expenditure side, decisions are clearly money influenced . . . by who has contributed to the candidates. . . . The price that the public pays for this process, whether it is in subsidies, taxes, or appropriations, is quite high."[15]

Most Congress members consider soliciting funds to be a somewhat humiliating experience—"begging for money." Yet even the most respected members of Congress must "make their calls" almost every day. They must telephone corporate executives, lobbyists, union chiefs, and executives of the special interests regulated by the committees on which they serve, and ask them for money. As they "dial for dollars," they must be careful not to state a quid pro quo of any kind. Yet, "by requesting campaign contributions from the special interests they will then regulate, they come as close to the solicitation of bribes as it is legally possible to get."[16]

It is perhaps a little less embarrassing to ask contributors to attend a fund-raising $1,000 luncheon or dinner:

> If you're on Ways and Means, like . . . some of my friends, anytime you want you can have a cozy little lunch downtown and tell them [the lobbyists] it's going to cost $1,000 or whatever it is, and the special interests flock—*flock*—to your luncheon.

> If they've got money in the bank, they know they have to give you a check. If the call comes in, it's tough for them to say no. That's why so many candidates are urged to get on the phone personally—because their campaign fund-raisers know that it's tougher to say no to the man himself.[17]

The ability to raise funds adds to the reputation for power of incumbent Congress members. Large war chests help deter challengers as well as reassure Washington policymakers that the incumbent will be staying in office. The 1974 Federal Election Commission Act, which, among other things, requires candidates to make public their campaign finances, actually creates an incentive to raise more funds. An unintended consequence of the act is to publicize the size of the candidate's campaign war chest; this publicity itself becomes a political asset for well-heeled incumbents. It signals to potential challengers that they face an uphill fight and might wisely consider staying out of the race.[18] And it signals to other contributors that the member is likely to stay in office and that they might want to stay in his or her good graces by adding further to the size of the money pile.

PRESIDENTIAL LEGITIMATION OF POLICY

The presidency lends legitimacy to government generally, more than to particular policy decisions. The president personifies American government for most people. In times of crisis, the American people look to the president to provide reassurance. It is the president who is expected to speak on behalf of people in times of national triumph and tragedy. The policy positions of president are *not* very closely tied to his popularity with the people.

It is true, of course, that presidents are expected to set forth policy initiatives in speeches, in messages to Congress (including the annual State of the

Union message), and in the annual *Budget of the United States Government*. In the course of preparing a White House legislative agenda, presidents and their chief advisers regularly sift through policies formulated in think tanks and policy planning organizations; developed in the offices of interest groups, law firms, and lobbyists; and suggested by heavy campaign contributors.

But the president's success in getting legislation enacted is closely tied to party control of Congress. Presidents are far more successful when they can work with a Congress controlled by their own party. Presidential "box scores"—the percentage of presidential initiatives and policies on which the president took a clear-cut position that are enacted into law by Congress—depend primarily on whether or not the president's party controls one or both houses of Congress (see figure 7.4). Democratic control of both houses of Congress resulted in significantly higher box scores for Democratic presidents John Kennedy, Lyndon Johnson, and Jimmy Carter than for Republican presidents Richard Nixon, Gerald Ford, and George Bush. Dwight Eisenhower and Ronald Reagan benefited from having Republican majorities in the Senate in their first terms, but they suffered when Democrats gained control of the Senate in their second terms. Bill Clinton was very successful in his first two years in office when the Democrats controlled Congress. But his box scores plummeted following the capture of Congress by Republicans in 1994.

Presidents are more successful in stopping legislation they oppose than in getting legislation they support passed by Congress. The veto power is the pres-

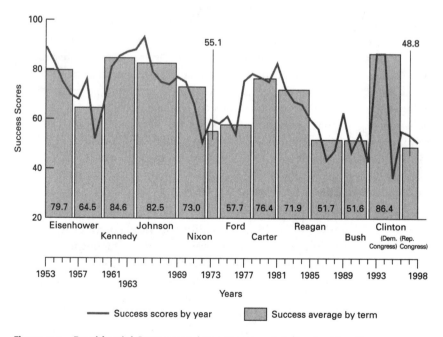

Figure 7.4 **Presidential Support and Congressional Policy Legitimation**

ident's most important weapon in dealing with Congress. Even the threat of the veto greatly enhances the president's legislative power. A bill vetoed by the president can be passed into law only by a two-thirds vote of both houses of Congress. Seldom is a president so weak that he cannot hold the loyalty of at least one-third of either the House or the Senate. From George Washington to Bill Clinton, more than 96 percent of all presidential vetoes have been sustained.

A president's signature on a bill is not only necessary for its enactment, but a president's support also adds to the legitimacy of the law.

JUDICIAL POLICY LEGITIMATION

Public policy in America is not fully legitimated until it has withstood judicial challenge. Increasingly, policies enacted by elected representatives in the United States are challenged in the courts. Legitimacy often must await a decision by an unelected federal court judge that actions by Congress and the president do not conflict with his or her interpretation of the Constitution of the United States.

The United States is unique among the democracies of the world in its reliance on courts to decide the most heated issues of American politics. As early as 1835 the French diplomat and traveler Alexis de Tocqueville observed: "There is hardly a political question in the United States which does not sooner or later journey into a judicial one." The Supreme Court of the United States has undertaken the lead in eliminating racial segregation, defining the limits of affirmative action, ensuring separation of church and state and deciding about prayer in schools, deciding about abortion, defining obscenity and pornography, ensuring equality of representation, defining the rights of criminal defendants, and even deciding the legitimacy of capital punishment.

Thus, courts not only function to legitimate the actions of other government decision makers by declaring their actions acceptable under the laws and Constitution of the United States, but they also undertake to make policy decisions themselves. And it has been argued that "in many ways, the decisions made by courts are more authoritative than other legitimating decisions, both because of the courts' connection to constitutional authority and because of the absence of any ready avenue of appeal once appeals through the court system are exhausted."[19]

Today, the power of federal courts to invalidate laws of Congress is widely accepted as legitimate. Yet this power—power of judicial review—is not specifically mentioned in the Constitution but has long been inferred from it. Alexander Hamilton wrote in 1787 that "limited government . . . can be preserved in practice no other way than through the medium of courts of justice, whose duty it is to declare all acts contrary to the manifest tenor of the Constitution void." But it was the historic decision of the Supreme Court in *Marbury* v. *Madison* in 1803 that established judicial review as a fundamental principle of American government. No serious challenge to the power of judicial review has arisen in American politics in more than a century.

Courts themselves help to ensure their own legitimacy in their special style of judicial decision making. Among the key elements in maintaining judicial legitimacy are the following:

- *An appearance of objectivity.* Because judges are not democratically elected but rather appointed for life, they endeavor to maintain the fiction that they are not engaged in policymaking at all but are merely "applying" the law or Constitution to specific cases.

- *The fiction of nonpartisanship.* Judges must not appear to allow political consideration to affect their decisions. Lawyers must not appear to "lobby" judges.

- *Special rules of access.* Federal courts act only in "cases and controversies" brought to them. They do not issue policy pronouncements in the absence of a case. They do not render advisory opinions to Congress or the president on pending legislation, or even after a law has been enacted, until a case comes before them that challenges the law.

- *A legalistic style.* Decorum in court proceedings is highly valued because it conveys a sense of dignity. Plaintiffs and defendants must present arguments to the courts in formal testimony, cross-examination, legal briefs, and oral presentations, all of which are highly ritualized.

These distinctive features of judicial decision making help to legitimize court decisions among both elites and masses.

CHAPTER 8

The Policy Implementation Process

I am impressed by the extent to which policymaking is dominated by the representatives of those bureaucracies and professions having a material stake in the management and funding of the intended policy and by those political staffs who see in a new program a chance for publicity, advancement, and a good reputation for their superiors.

—JAMES Q. WILSON

"IMPLEMENTATION IS THE continuation of politics by other means."[1] The policymaking process continues well after a law has been passed by Congress and signed by the president. The focus of the process merely shifts from Capitol Hill and the White House to the Washington bureaucracy—to the myriad of departments, agencies, and bureaus of the federal executive branch of government that are charged with the task of implementing the law.

The actual governance of the nation rests in the hands of bureaucrats. Neither Congress nor the president collects taxes (the task of the Internal Revenue Service), or closes down nuclear power plants (the Nuclear Regulatory Commission), or halts commercial development on wetlands (the Environmental Protection Agency), or inspects factories for safety violations (the Occupational Safety and Health Administration), or grants licenses to television stations (the Federal Communications Commission), or orders employers to hire minorities (the Equal Employment Opportunity Commission), and so on. Approximately 2,000 federal government agencies have rulemaking power. Bureaucracies announce an estimated *twenty* rules or regulations for every one law of Congress.[2]

Policy implementation is all of the activities designed to carry out the laws enacted by the legislative branch of government. These activities may include the creation of new organizations—departments, agencies, bureaus, and so on—to carry out new laws, or the assignment of new responsibilities to existing organizations. These activities may include the development of specific rules and regulations that interpret the real meaning of laws, and they almost always include the making of budgets and hiring of personnel, spending money, and performing specified tasks. And these activities often include the adjudication of individual cases—deciding whether a person, firm, or corporation has complied with laws and regulations and, if not, what penalties or corrective actions are to be imposed.

TOP-DOWN POLICY IMPLEMENTATION

In theory, bureaucracies function in a top-down fashion. It was the German sociologist Max Weber who *defined* bureaucracy as (1) a chain of command (hierarchy); (2) a division of labor among subunits (specialization); (3) specification of authority (span of control); (4) adaptation of structure, authority, and rules to the organization's goals (goal orientation); (5) impersonality in executing tasks (neutrality); and (6) predictability of behavior (standardization).[3] Thus, bureaucracies are not designed to be democratic institutions themselves, but rather to be hierarchical organizations that function to carry out policies decided by higher government authorities (see figure 8.1). In a democracy, the bureaucracy is supposed to carry out policies decided by representatives of the people.

But the problem of ensuring the responsiveness of bureaucracies to higher authorities, in both democratic and authoritarian regimes, has plagued governments for centuries. (The familiar bureaucratic term *red tape* derives its meaning from the reddish tape used by seventeenth century kings and courts to bind documents. Unwrapping these documents entangled one in red tape.) Today, the president, White House staff, and cabinet officials spend a great deal of their time and energy trying to control the bureaucracy over which they have constitutional authority.

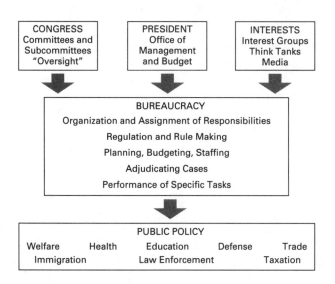

Figure 8.1   Top-Down Policy Implementation

And in Congress and its committees, "oversight" has become a common theme. Certainly "the people" have no direct control over bureaucratic actions. Most people have come to view bureaucracy as impersonal, insensitive, and unresponsive to their needs (see feature: "Mass Distrust of Government Bureaucracies").

FEATURE: MASS DISTRUST OF GOVERNMENT BUREAUCRACIES

The American people believe that the federal government has too much power. Among the federal government's many bureaucracies, the U.S. military is the most highly respected. More than 80 percent of Americans believe that the military has about the right amount or not enough power (see table).

Mass Distrust of Government Bureaucracies

Q: As I read off the following, please tell me whether you think it has too much power in the United States today, about the right amount power, or not enough power.

	Too Much	About Right	Not Enough
The federal government in Washington	20%	29%	8%
The Internal Revenue Service	63	32	3
The Central Intelligence Agency	42	37	9
The Bureau of Alcohol, Tobacco, and Firearms	39	34	23
The Federal Bureau of Investigation	32	48	16
The military	17	57	23

Source: Gallup poll, 1995.

But most other federal agencies fare poorly in popular opinion polls. Clearly the most detested federal agency is the tax-collecting Internal Revenue Service; 63 percent of Americans believe that it has too much power. The power of the Central Intelligence Agency (CIA) as well as the Bureau of Alcohol, Tobacco, and Firearms (ATF) also appear to raise concern among many Americans, perhaps in part because of adverse publicity incurred by these agencies in recent years. (The CIA was deeply embarrassed in 1994 by the revelation that a high officer had been paid millions of dollars by Russian agents to work secretly on their behalf and expose U.S. agents to danger and death; the ATF was strongly criticized for attacking the Branch Davidian compound near Waco, Texas, in 1993 and causing numerous deaths.)

SOURCES OF BUREAUCRATIC POWER

How has the bureaucracy come to exercise so much power in American society? Why has control of the bureaucracy become such a central concern of both masses and elites?

Bureaucracies grow in size and gain in power with advances in technology, increases in information, and growth in the size and complexity of society. Large, complex democracies cannot be governed directly by their elected representatives. Neither the president nor Congress can involve themselves in the virtually endless details of regulating nuclear power plants, or monitoring environmental threats, or defining factory safety violations, or allocating broadcast channels, or investigating complaints of discrimination, or even attempting to interpret the 9,400 pages of the U.S. Tax Code, which Congress itself passed and the president signed.

The power of the bureaucracy is also enhanced when Congress and the president deliberately shift policymaking responsibility from themselves to the bureaucrats. Frequently Congress and the president enact laws largely for symbolic purposes—laws that are vague and ambiguous, for example, laws that require that prescription drugs be "safe and effective," laws that prevent employers from engaging in "unfair labor practices," laws that guarantee "equal employment opportunity." Bureaucrats are given the authority in these symbolic laws and phrases to decide what actually will be done. Indeed, reassuring the public of Congress's and the president's concern about environmental protection, occupational safety, fair employment, and so on, and then turning over actual governance to bureaucrats, serves the political purposes of elected officials very well. If implementing regulations turns out to be unpopular, Congress and the president can blame the bureaucrats.

The internal dynamics of bureaucratic governance also expands bureaucratic power. Bureaucracies regularly press for increases in their own size and budgets and for additions to their own regulatory authority. Rarely do bureaucrats request a reduction in their authority, the elimination of a program, or a decrease in their agency's budget or personnel. Instead, over time, "budget maximization" becomes the driving force in government bureaucracies.[4] Bureaucrats, like everyone else, seek higher pay, greater job security, and more power and authority for themselves.

Finally, bureaucratic expansionism is facilitated by the "incremental" nature of most policymaking.[5] Bureaucrats are seldom required to defend the entire purpose of their agency or program. To do so each year at budget time, for example, would require policymakers to reconsider virtually every policy or program established over the years. Neither Congress nor the White House has the time or energy to reconsider systematically the value of each one of the thousands of federal agencies and programs on an annual basis. Nor do they wish to refight past political battles every year. So they focus active consideration on bureaucratic requests for *new or expanded* authority, programs, and budgets. When new needs, services, or functions are identified, they do not displace older ones but instead simply are added to those already being performed by the bureaucracy. The result is that many programs, services, and expenditures continue long after there is any real justification for them. The bureaucracy simply expands to accommodate new demands.

BUREAUCRATIC ORGANIZATION

The executive branch of the United States government—"the Washington bureaucracy"—consists of about 2.8 million civilian employees, organized into fourteen departments, sixty independent agencies and government corporations, and a large Executive Office of the President (see figure 8.2, p. 142).

Cabinet departments are hierarchically organized, each headed by a secretary (with the exception of the Justice Department, which is headed by the Attorney General) who is appointed by the president and confirmed by the Senate. The Cabinet rarely functions as a group. It consists of the secretaries of the fourteen departments, the vice president, the UN ambassador, the CIA director, and the Special Trade Representative, with the president as its head. Presidents hold Cabinet meetings not to decide policy, but to emphasize their views to their principal executive officers.

The power and prestige of Cabinet members varies not only by the size and budget of their departments, but also by the importance of the function that they perform. The traditional "pecking order" of departments and prestige rankings of their secretaries was determined by their date of origin. Thus, the Departments of State, Treasury, Defense (originally separate War and Navy Departments), and Justice head the protocol list of departments.

The creation of a Cabinet department confers legitimacy on a governmental function and prestige on its secretary. The elevation of an executive agency to Cabinet-level status reflects the political judgment of the president and Congress that a particular function of government ought to be emphasized. Pressures from "client" interest groups (interest groups principally served by the department)—as well as presidential and congressional desire to pose as defenders and promoters of the groups' interests—have led to the creation of most of the newer departments. Thus, for example, President Lyndon B. Johnson created the Department of Housing and Urban Development to demonstrate his concern about problems of inner cities and their residents in the turbulent 1960s. President Jimmy Carter sought the support of teachers' unions and educational administrators by creating a separate Department of Education in 1979; he simultaneously changed the name of the Department of Health, Education, and Welfare to the Department of Health and Human Services (presumably "human services" is a more politically acceptable phrase than "welfare"). President Ronald Reagan promised to cut the size of the federal bureaucracy and even to eliminate the Departments of Energy and Education. But nothing arouses the fighting instincts of bureaucrats more than the threat of deemphasizing their program; Reagan's plans were derailed by the combined power of the energy industry, teachers' unions, and the educational establishment.

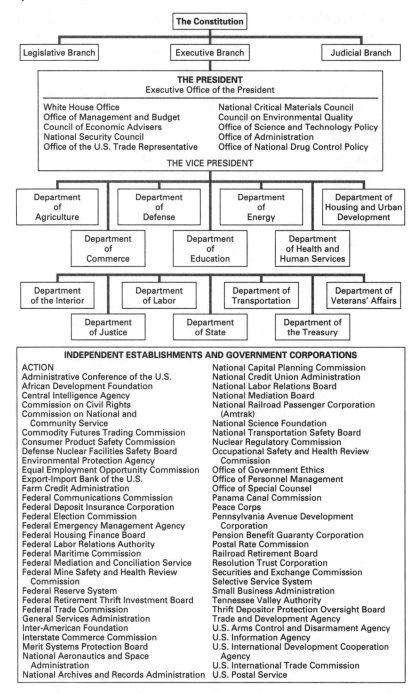

Figure 8.2   U.S. Government Organization Chart

Source: Chart prepared by U.S. Bureau of the Census.

But Reagan was successful in elevating the Veterans Administration to the Department of Veterans' Affairs. President Bill Clinton promised to elevate the Environmental Protection Agency to a Cabinet department, but he never generated the political support needed to do so.

BUREAUCRATIC RESPONSIVENESS

The president's power to appoint and remove most top executive officers would seem to ensure policy responsiveness of the bureaucracy. Yet many obstacles to responsiveness remain. The U.S. Constitution (Article II, Section 2) gives the president power to "appoint Ambassadors, other public Ministers and Consuls, Judges of the Supreme Court, and all other Officers of the United States" with the "Advice and Consent of the Senate." Traditionally, the Senate routinely confirmed presidential Cabinet appointments, on the theory that presidents were entitled to make their own mistakes in their own administrations. But in recent years, the Senate confirmation process has become increasingly partisan. In 1989 the Senate rejected President Bush's nomination of John Tower as Secretary of Defense in a bruising partisan battle that included charges that the former U.S. senator from Texas was a heavy drinker. In 1993 President Clinton was obliged to withdraw the nomination of Zoë Baird as Attorney General following charges that she employed an illegal alien as a baby-sitter. The intense public scrutiny now focused on presidential nominees for high public office, together with financial disclosure and conflict-of-interest laws, make it difficult for presidents to recruit top people for cabinet posts.

Civil Service

Most federal employees are career civil servants. The president actually appoints people to only about 2,500 positions, of which only about 600 can be considered policymaking positions. Often presidential appointments fall to career civil servants by default because the president cannot find qualified political appointees.

Bureaucratic responsiveness to the president, and to presidentially appointed department and agency heads, remains a central problem in public administration. More than 90 percent of federal employees are protected in their jobs by civil service or other merit systems. Although the Office of Personnel Management is headed by a single director appointed by the president, an independent Merit Systems Protection Board hears appeals by federal employees regarding disciplinary actions. After a brief probationary period, a federal employee cannot be dismissed except for "cause." Severe obstacles to dismissing a federal employee have resulted in a rate of dismissal substantially below that of any sector of private employment.

Bureaucratic "Culture"

Departments, agencies, and bureaus tend to develop their own "culture" over time, usually in strong support of the governmental function and client group served. It is extremely difficult for a presidential administration to change an agency's culture, especially when attempting to reduce its resources, functions, or services. Inasmuch as a majority of career bureaucrats are Democrats, this problem is accentuated in Republican administrations. Political heads of agencies, placed there by a presidential administration, can often be outwitted by career bureaucrats who know they will continue to be in their jobs long after their political boss is gone. (In recent administrations, the average tenure of a Cabinet member has been only about two and one-half years.) And some political heads have been known to "go native"—that is, yield to the culture of the agency itself, promote its interests, and give priority to its client groups over presidential policy preferences.

The culture of a bureaucracy includes beliefs about the value of the agency's functions and importance of serving the agency's principal clients, whether they be agricultural interests, public schools, social workers, the elderly, civil rights groups, environmental groups, or the defense industry. Bureaucrats believe their work is important, and they resist efforts to reduce the activities, size, or budget of their agency.[6] Rather, bureaucrats generally support the enlargement of the public sector, whether in agriculture, education, welfare, Social Security and Medicare, civil rights, environmental protection, or the military services. Most government agencies are dominated by people who have spent most of their lives in government service in the same field. They share a close association with the agency's client groups and political supporters. Their loyalty lies principally with the bureaucracy in which they serve, rather than with the president or Congress.

Implementation requires the responsiveness of government bureaucracies, yet responsiveness is often difficult to achieve. The executive branch of the United States government is a massive, complex, and confusing set of organizations. Most of these organizations have their own goals and constituencies. While bureaucracy is formally organized as a hierarchical "top-down" system, the barriers to effective implementation of public policy, even for elites, are substantial.

BUREAUCRATIC REGULATION

Bureaucratic regulation is central to the policymaking process. Formal bureaucratic rules and regulations have the *force of law*—bureaucracies may levy fines and penalties for violations of these regulations, and these fines and penalties are enforceable in federal courts. Congress itself can only amend or repeal a formal regulation by passing a new law and obtaining the president's signature. Bureaucratic regulations (policy) may remain in effect despite popular opposition when Congress is slow to respond, when legislation is blocked by congressional committee members, or when the president supports the bureaucracy and refuses to sign bills overturning regulations. The courts seldom overturn bureaucratic regulations unless they exceed the authority granted to the agency by law or unless the agency has not followed the proper procedure in adopting them. (The Administrative Procedures Act requires agencies to announce proposed regulations in the *Federal Register*; hold hearings allowing presentation of evidence and arguments regarding the proposed regulations; solicit "public comments," usually the arguments of interest groups; consult with the Office of Management and Budget; and publish all new regulations in the *Federal Register.*) Many regulatory commissions are *independent,* that is, they are located organizationally outside executive departments, and their members are appointed for long terms by a president who has little control over their actions. A list of the major regulatory commissions is provided in table 8.1 (p. 146).

Each year federal regulatory bureaucracies issue thousands of rules and regulations, conduct thousands of inspections, investigate thousands of complaints, require businesses to submit hundreds of thousands of forms, hold thousands of hearings to determine "compliance" or "noncompliance," issue thousands of corrective orders, and levy thousands of fines and penalties. Federal regulatory bureaucracies are legislators, investigators, prosecutors, and judges—all wrapped into one.

Historically, federal regulatory bureaucracies arose as an elite response to mass discontent. (The first federal regulatory bureaucracy, the Interstate Commerce Commission, was created in 1887 to reassure Midwest farmers that railroads would not overcharge them.) But the reform movements that led to the establishment of many of the older regulatory agencies frequently lost influence over these agencies, and the regulators were "captured" by the regulated industries. These industries came to benefit from government regulation: by acting against the most wayward firms in an industry, the regulatory agencies improve the public's image of the industry as a whole and provide the masses with reassurance that the industry is behaving properly. By limiting entry into an industry by smaller firms (either directly, by denying them routes or broadcast channels, for example, or indirectly, by increasing the costs of doing business), the regulatory commissions reduce competition. This grants advantage to larger, well-established corporations by curtailing the prospects of success by newer, cheaper, cut-rate competitors. Among the traditional regulatory agencies thought to be in partnership with their regulated industries are the Federal Communications Commission (FCC, with the communications industry, including the television networks); the Securities and Exchange Commission (SEC, with the investment firms and stock market); the Federal Reserve Board (FRB, with the banking industry); the National Labor Relations Board (NLRB, with the nation's major labor unions). The airline industry strongly *opposed* the 1978 reduction of the Civil Aeronautics Board's (CAB) power to allocate airline routes and set rates. The CAB went out of existence in 1985, and the airline industry was "set free" against its will to engage in competition over routes and rates. Also during the 1980s, the Interstate Commerce Commission was first stripped of its power to set railroad and trucking rates, and it was finally abolished in 1995. But *deregulation* has been limited. It threatens bureaucratic power, diminishes the influence of lawyers and lobbyists, and forces industries to become more competitive.

Regulatory activity expands each year.[7] Particularly active are the Environ-

Table 8.1 Major U.S. Government Regulatory Bureaucracies

Commission	Date Created	Primary Functions
Federal Reserve Board (FRB)	1913	Regulates the nation's money supply by making monetary policy, which influences the lending and investing activities of commercial banks and the cost and availability of money and credit
Federal Trade Commission (FTC)	1914	Regulates business to prohibit unfair methods of competition and unfair or deceptive acts or practices
Food and Drug Administration (FDA)	1930	Sets standards of safety and efficacy for foods, drugs, and medical devices
Federal Home Loan Bank	1932	Regulates savings and loan associations that specialize in making home mortgage loans
Federal Communications Commission (FCC)	1934	Regulates interstate and foreign communications by radio, television, wire, and cable
Securities and Exchange Commission (SEC)	1934	Regulates the securities and financial markets (such as the stock market)
National Labor Relations Board (NLRB)	1935	Protects employees' rights to organize; prevents unfair labor practices
Federal Maritime Commission	1961	Regulates the waterborne foreign and domestic offshore commerce of the United States
Equal Employment Opportunity Commission (EEOC)	1964	Investigates and rules on charges of racial, gender, and age discrimination by employers and unions, in all aspects of employment
Environmental Protection Agency (EPA)	1970	Issues and enforces pollution control standards regarding air, water, solid waste, pesticides, radiation, and toxic substances
Occupational Safety and Health Administration (OSHA)	1970	Issues workplace regulations; investigates, cites, and penalizes for noncompliance
Consumer Product Safety Commission (CPSC)	1972	Protects the public against product-related deaths, illnesses, and injuries
Commodity Futures Trading Commission	1974	Regulates trading on the futures exchanges as well as the activities of commodity exchange members, public brokerage houses, commodity salespersons, trading advisers, and pool operators
Nuclear Regulatory Commission (NRC)	1974	Regulates and licenses the users of nuclear energy

Table 8.1 *(continued)*

Commission	Date Created	Primary Functions
Federal Energy Regulatory Commission (formerly Federal Power Commission)	1977	Regulates the transportation and sale of natural gas, the transmission and sale of electricity, the licensing of hydroelectric power projects, and the transportation of oil by pipeline

Source: The United States Government Manual 1996/97 (Washington, D.C.: Government Printing Office, 1997).

mental Protection Agency (EPA) with its growing seventeen-volume set of regulations; the Occupational Safety and Health Administration (OSHA) with its power to regulate, investigate, cite, and penalize employers for workplace violations; and the Equal Employment Opportunity Commission (EEOC) with its power to issue orders regarding the racial and gender makeup of a workforce and cite and penalize employers for violation of its orders. Unlike other regulatory bureaucracies, these agencies extend their jurisdiction to all industries. These "activist" agencies often pose serious problems for small businesses that cannot afford to allocate resources to "comply" with their orders or to incur the legal fees required to challenge them. In contrast, large corporations have the resources to either comply with or confront these agencies. Large corporations can afford to conduct "environmental impact" studies, to put in place workplace safety programs, and to establish their own corporate "affirmative action" bureaucracies. In short, corporate America has come to terms with, and generally has come to support the goals of these activist agencies. The cost of all this regulation is borne mainly by the American public, and most of these regulatory costs are currently hidden from the American public.[8]

No regulatory bureaucracy is as powerful or independent as the Federal Reserve System (see feature: "The Fed: Money Is Too Important to Be Left to Democratic Governments," pp. 148–50). Most economically developed nations have central banks whose principal responsibility is to regulate the supply of money. And most of these nations have found it best to remove this responsibility from the direct control of democratically elected officials. Politicians everywhere are sorely tempted to inflate the supply of money in order to fund projects and programs with newly created money rather than taxes. The result, of course, is usually inflation—a general rise in prices—sometimes to the point of making money virtually worthless. But early in the twentieth century, the American banking community convinced Congress and President Woodrow Wilson to delegate the constitutional power "to Coin Money and Regulate the Value Thereof" (Article I, Section 8) to a fully independent bureaucracy.

FEATURE: THE FED: MONEY IS TOO IMPORTANT TO BE LEFT TO DEMOCRATIC GOVERNMENTS

The nation's money supply is far too important to be left to democratic institutions. It became apparent at the beginning of the twentieth century that the control of money would have to be removed from direct government control and placed in the hands of bankers themselves. Moreover, it was generally agreed that bankers' power over money would have to be unrestricted by Congress or the president.

The Federal Reserve Act of 1913 created the Federal Reserve System. Its purpose is to decide on the nation's monetary policy and credit conditions, to supervise and regulate all banking activity, and to provide various services to banks. Federal Reserve banks are banks' banks; only banks may open accounts at Federal Reserve Banks.

The Federal Reserve System is fully independent—its decisions need not be ratified by the president, Congress, the courts, or any other governmental institution. It does not depend on annual federal appropriations, but instead it finances itself. Theoretically, Congress could amend or repeal the Federal Reserve Act of 1913, but to do so would be economically unthinkable. The only changes to the Act throughout the century have been to *add* to the powers of "the Fed." In the International Banking Act of 1978, the Fed was directed by the Congress to encourage economic growth, maintain high levels of employment, keep inflation low, and maintain moderate long-term interest rates.

Controlling the Money Supply. Banks create money when they make loans. They simply create "demand deposits" and make them available to borrowers. Currency (cash) in circulation, together with demand deposits, constitute the nation's principal money supply—"M1." Demand deposits far exceed currency in circulation. (Only about 5 percent of the money supply is in the form of cash.) Most money transactions consist of checks or electronic transfers; in normal times people are satisfied to accept these paper or electronic promises of banks in lieu of currency. But at times in the past, large numbers of people have demanded that their deposits be given to them in currency—creating a "run" on a bank. Inasmuch as the bank simply created these deposits, it cannot possibly pay all of its depositors (or even a significant portion of them) in currency. The bank fails, and depositors lose their money.

The Federal Reserve System was created by bankers primarily to stabilize the banking system and control the supply of money. The Fed requires all banks to maintain a reserve in currency or in deposits with a Federal

Reserve Bank. If the "reserve ratio" is set at 20 percent, for example, a bank may only create demand deposits up to five times the amount of its reserve. (If it has $100 million in reserve, its total demand deposits cannot exceed $500 million.)

If the Fed decides that there is too much money in the economy (inflation), it can raise the reserve requirement, for example from 20 to 25 percent, reducing what a bank can create in demand deposits to only four times its reserve. (If a bank has $100 million in reserve, its total demand deposits would be limited to $400 million.) In this way the Fed can expand or contract money supply as it sees fit.

The Fed can also alter the money supply by changing the interest it charges member banks to borrow reserve. A bank can expand its deposits by borrowing reserve from the Fed, but it must pay the Fed an interest rate, called the "discount rate," in order to do so. The Fed regularly raises and lowers the discount rate, thereby making it easier or harder for banks to borrow reserve. Raising the discount rate tends to contract money supply; lowering it expands the money supply.

The Fed is also authorized to buy and sell U.S. Treasury bonds and notes in what is called "open market operations." Indeed, the assets of the Fed consist of U.S. bonds and notes. Each day the Open Market Desk of the Fed buys and sells billions of dollars worth of government bonds. If it sells more than it buys, it reduces its own reserve and hence its ability to lend reserve to banks; this contracts the money supply. If it buys more than it sells, it adds to its own reserve, enabling it to lend reserve to member banks and expand the money supply.

Fed Governance. The governance of the Fed ensures its isolation from democratic politics. Its Board of Governors is made up of seven members appointed by the president and confirmed by the Senate. The full term of a member is *fourteen years*, however, and appointments are staggered so that one expires in each even-numbered year. The chairman of the board is appointed for a four-year term starting midway through each presidential term. This ensures that the new president cannot immediately install a new chairman. Each Federal Reserve Bank has its own board of nine directors chosen by member banks. All meetings of the Fed are held in secret.

Alan Greenspan: Ruling the Money Supply. Alan Greenspan was first appointed chairman of the Federal Reserve Board in 1987 by President Ronald Reagan. Greenspan replaced the long-serving chair Paul Volcker, whose tight-money policies in the early 1980s ultimately brought down the high rates of inflation that had plagued the nation for most of the 1970s. Volcker went on to serve as chairman of the World Bank. Greenspan's first test came in late 1987 when the U.S. stock market plunged dramatically. He quickly acted to ensure that Federal Reserve Banks would have enough cash on hand to prevent panic. During the 1991 recession, Greenspan pushed interest rates down to a twenty-year low and cut the reserve requirement in half in order to expand the money supply. Since then, Greenspan has worked diligently to keep inflation low even during the booming economy of the 1990s.

BUREAUCRATIC BUDGET MAKING

The budget is the single most important policy statement of any government. It is true that governments do many things that do not appear on the budget, and that governments often try to shift the costs of their activities off the budget. But the budget tells us how much money is being spent by government and for what it is being spent.

Overall, federal government expenditures currently amount to about 20 percent of the U.S. gross domestic product (GDP), the sum of all the goods and services produced in the United States in a year and a common measure of the size of the American economy. (State and local governments spend an additional 10 percent of the GDP, bringing the total governmental portion of the GDP to about 30 percent.) After decades of rapid growth of federal government spending relative to the size of the economy (from 1930 to 1980 federal spending grew from 8 percent to 22 percent of the GDP), federal spending has leveled out and even declined slightly relative to the economy (see figure 8.3). But this apparent success in controlling the growth of government is attributable primarily to the dramatic growth in the American economy in the late 1990s. In recent years, federal spending has not grown as rapidly as the economy. Nonetheless, federal spending is nearing the $2 *trillion* mark.

Formal Processes

The president is responsible for the preparation of the *Budget of the United States Government* each year. (The president was first given this responsibility in the Budget and Accounting Act of 1921 developed by the Brookings Institution.) But Congress ultimately controls the purse strings; the Constitution (Article I, Section 9) is very explicit: "No Money shall be drawn from the Treasury, but in Consequence of Appropriations made by Law." The president relies on the Office of Management and Budget (OMB) to prepare the budget for consideration by Congress. The OMB reviews the budget requests of all executive department and agencies, adjusting them

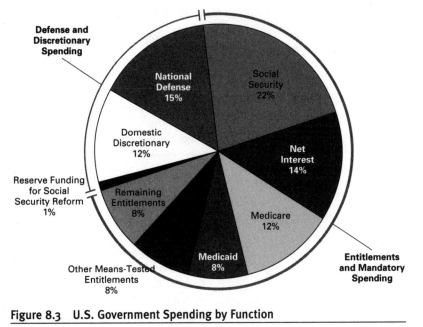

Figure 8.3   U.S. Government Spending by Function

Source: Budget of the U.S. Government, Fiscal Year 2000.

to fit the president's overall policy goals. It is the OMB that actually prepares the *Budget of the United States Government* each fiscal year for transmittal to the Congress. The formal budgetary process is outlined in table 8.2 (p. 152).

The president's budget is initially sent to the House and Senate Budget Committees, which are responsible for drafting a "budget resolution" for approval by Congress, setting ceilings for appropriations in various areas. The House and Senate Budget Committees rely on their own bureaucracy, the Congressional Budget Office (CBO), to review recommendations made by the president and the OMB. (The House and Senate Budget Committees and the CBO were established in the Budget and Impoundment Control Act of 1974, another contribution of the Brookings Institution.) Congress is supposed to pass a budget resolution by late spring; the resolution is supposed to guide the House and Senate Appropriations Committees in writing the actual appropriations acts. If the Appropriations Committees bring bills to the floor that exceed the ceilings established by the budget resolution, Congress must prepare a "reconciliation bill" to reconcile the amounts set by the Budget Committees with those of the Appropriations Committees. When passed, the reconciliation bill binds the Appropriations Committees and the Congress to ceilings in each area. Congress regularly considers thirteen separate appropriations bills, each one covering a broad functional area of government, for example, defense, education, human

Table 8.2 U.S. Government Formal Budgetary Process

Approximate Schedule	Actors	Tasks
PRESIDENTIAL BUDGET MAKING		
January–March	President and OMB	The Office of Management and Budget presents long-range forecasts for revenues and expenditures to the president. The president and the OMB develop general guidelines for all federal agencies. Agencies are sent guidelines and forms for their budget requests.
April–July	Executive agencies	Agencies prepare and submit budget requests to the OMB.
August–October	OMB and agencies	The OMB reviews agent requests and holds hearings with agency officials. The OMB usually tries to reduce agency requests.
November–December	OMB and president	The OMB presents revised budget to president. Occasionally agencies may appeal OMB decisions directly to the president. The president and the OMB write budget messages for Congress.
January	President	The president presents budget for the next fiscal year to Congress.
CONGRESSIONAL BUDGET PROCESS		
February–May	CBO and Congress	Standing committees review taxing and spending proposals for reports to House and Senate Budget Committees. The Congressional Budget Office (CBO) also reviews entire presidential budget and reports to Budget Committees.
May–June	Congress; House and Senate Budget Committees	House and Senate Budget Committees present first concurrent resolution, which sets overall total for budget outlays in major categories. Full House and Senate vote on resolution. Committees are instructed to stay within Budget Committee's resolution.
July–September	Congress, House and Senate Appropriations Committees and Budget Committees	House and Senate Appropriations Committees and subcommittees draw up detailed appropriations bills. Bills are submitted to House and Senate Budget Committees for second concurrent resolution. Budget Committees may force reductions through "reconciliation" provisions to limit spending. The full House and Senate vote on "reconciliations" and second (firm) concurrent resolution.

Table 8.2 *(continued)*

Approximate Schedule	Actors	Tasks
September-October	Congress and president	The House and Senate pass various appropriations bills (nine to sixteen bills, by major functional category, such as "defense"). Each is sent to the president for signature. (If vetoed by the president, the appropriations bills go back to House and Senate, which must override veto with two-thirds vote in each body or revise bills to gain president's approval).
EXECUTIVE BUDGET IMPLEMENTATION		
After 1 October	Congress and president	Fiscal year for all federal agencies begins 1 October. If no appropriations bill has been passed by Congress and signed by the president for an agency, Congress must pass and the president sign a "continuing resolution" to allow the agency to spend at the previous year's level until a new appropriations act is passed. If no continuing resolution is passed, the agency must officially cease spending government funds and must officially shut down.

services, commerce, state, judiciary, and so on. Like all other legislation, appropriations bills must be passed in identical form in both houses of Congress. All appropriations acts should be passed by Congress before the beginning of each fiscal year, 1 October, but Congress rarely meets this deadline. Since the Constitution prohibits the expenditure of any funds not appropriated by Congress, federal bureaucracies theoretically must shut down if Congress does not pass an appropriations act for them before the beginning of the fiscal year. To avoid this problem, Congress usually passes a "continuing resolution" authorizing government agencies to continue spending money for a specified period of time, allowing Congress additional time to pass an appropriations act.

Incrementalism

The formal budgetary process tends to obscure how government budgets are actually determined. In reality, budgeting is an "incremental" process. Decision makers in both the White House and Congress do *not* systematically reexamine the value of every program and activity each year in preparing the budget. Instead, decision makers generally use last year's agency and program expenditures as a *base* that is accepted as legitimate, focusing their attention on new items and requested increases over last year's base. An agency's budget is seldom ever reviewed as a whole; an agency is rarely required to defend or explain activities or expenditures that have been approved in the past. But requested increases *do* require justification, and they are subject to scrutiny and possible reduction by the OMB or Congress. In practice, this incremental decision-making process means that most agencies can expect to receive in any year approximately what they received in previous years, plus a little more to account for inflation and growth in the numbers of people they are expected to serve.

Incremental policymaking has sometimes been portrayed as nonrational. That is, incremental decision making does *not* involve an annual review of societal goals, an exploration of the wide range of policy alternatives, research into the benefits and costs of each of these alternatives, and the selection of the alternative that provides maximum benefits with minimum costs. Incremental policymaking recognizes the impractical aspects of "rational-comprehensive" policymaking, and it describes and even recommends a more limited approach to policymaking.

Advocates of incremental policymaking argue that over the long run it may turn out to be actually *more* rational than the "rational-comprehensive" model of policymaking. First, it reduces the costs of decision making—the time, energy, and political conflict that is likely to accompany a comprehensive annual review of all possible policy alternatives. Second, it provides a base of experience with past policies and knowledge of the likely consequences of continuing in the same direction. It minimizes the possibility that new and untried policy alternatives will lead to damaging unintended consequences. It is safer to stick with known programs when the consequences of new programs cannot be accurately predicted. Finally, incrementalism reduces the need to make major changes in programs each year and thus reduces the costs of change. Governments usually have heavy investments in existing programs (sunk costs) which preclude major change. These costs may be in equipment, buildings, or other tangible items, and they may also be found in psychological dispositions, administrative practices, and organizational structure. Changes almost always involve dislocations of various kinds, personal as well as bureaucratic.

It should be noted, however, that a series of annual budgetary increases for an agency or program can result in major policy shifts over time. For example, spending for Social Security was only about 5 percent of the federal budget in 1960, but today Social Security spending is about 23 percent of the budget, even though no major changes were made in the program in the intervening years. Likewise, Medicare expenditures have risen from about 3 percent of the budget in 1970 to more than 12 percent today, without any major overhaul of the Medicare program. National defense spending suffered "decrements" in spending over time; 1970 defense spending was 42 percent of the federal budget compared to only 15 percent today. And reductions in defense spending began

Table 8.3   Changing Patterns of U.S. Government Spending

Function	1960	1965	1970	1975	1980	1985	1991	1998	2001
				BILLIONS OF DOLLARS					
National defense	45.9	49.6	81.7	86.5	134.0	252.7	273.3	259.4	291.2
Income security[a]	3.7	9.1	15.6	50.2	86.5	128.2	170.8	247.5	259.7
Social Security	4.3	16.4	30.3	64.7	118.5	188.6	269.0	384.3	425.7
Medicare	—	—	6.2	12.7	32.1	65.8	104.5	207.1	220.5
Health[b]	0.8	1.8	5.9	12.9	23.2	33.5	71.2	138.2	166.7
Agriculture	3.3	4.8	5.2	3.0	8.8	25.6	15.2	12.3	22.4
Natural resources	1.0	2.1	3.1	7.3	13.9	13.4	18.6	22.3	24.9
Veterans' benefits	5.4	5.1	8.7	16.6	21.2	26.3	31.3	41.0	46.4
Interest on debt	8.3	10.4	14.4	23.2	52.5	129.4	194.5	249.9	208.3
All other[c]	9.5	16.1	26.6	55.2	100.2	73.8	174.6	166.0	169.2
Total	92.2	118.3	195.6	332.3	590.9	912.8	1,323.0	1687.5	1,835.0
				PERCENTAGE DISTRIBUTION					
National defense	55.8	43.0	41.8	26.0	22.7	26.7	20.6	15.3	15.8
Income security[a]	4.5	7.9	8.0	15.1	14.6	13.5	129.0	14.6	14.1
Social Security	5.2	14.2	15.5	19.5	20.1	19.9	20.3	22.8	23.2
Medicare	0.0	0.0	3.2	3.8	5.4	7.0	7.9	12.2	12.0
Health[b]	0.9	1.5	3.0	3.9	3.9	3.5	5.4	8.1	9.1
Agriculture	4.0	4.2	2.7	0.9	1.5	2.7	1.1	0.7	1.2
Natural resources	1.2	1.8	1.6	2.2	2.4	1.4	1.4	1.3	1.4
Veterans' benefits	6.6	4.4	4.4	5.0	3.6	2.8	2.4	2.4	2.5
Interest on debt	10.1	9.0	7.4	7.0	8.9	13.7	14.7	14.8	11.4
All other[c]	11.0	13.3	12.0	15.7	15.3	8.2	13.2	9.7	9.3
Total	100.0	100.0	100.0	100.0	100.0	100.0	100.0	100.0	100.0

Sources: Statistical Abstract of the United States 1999 and *The Budget of the United States Government, Fiscal Year 2001.*

a. This includes public assistance, food stamps, railroad and government employee retirement benefits, and unemployment compensation.

b. This includes medical, health, research, and occupational health and safety.

c. This includes international affairs, science, space, transportation, education, energy, commerce, community development, justice, and general government.

in 1985, well before the end of the Cold War. In short, incremental policymaking does *not* preclude major changes in policy over time.

Incrementalism in federal budget making is driven primarily by "uncontrollable" entitlement programs. These are programs established by Congress in the past and considered as commitments in future federal budgets. Federal programs that provide classes of people with legally enforceable claims on govern-ment funds are called "entitlement" programs. Entitlement programs now account for well more than half of all federal spending, including Social Secu-rity, Medicare and Medicaid, food stamps, federal employees' retirement, and veterans' benefits. These programs provide benefits that past Congresses have pledged the federal government to provide. They are not really "uncontrollable"; Congress can always amend the basic laws that established them. But this is extremely difficult to do politically; it might be regarded by the voters as a fail-ure of trust. And, of course, the federal government is obliged to pay interest on the national debt, that is, to pay interest on government bonds.

The result of the incremental expansion of entitlement spending over time has been a gradual reduction in so-called discretionary spending. But "discre-tionary" is a misnomer for most of the programs categorized as such. It includes everything from funding federal courts, prisons, and law-enforcement agencies, to paying for air traffic control, the Coast Guard, tax collection, and even the costs incurred by Congress itself. In other words, very little of this "discretionary" spending is truly discretionary. The result is that the White House and Congress give serious consideration each year to only a very small proportion of the total federal budget.

BUREAUCRATIC ADJUDICATION

Policy implementation also involves bureaucratic decisions about individual cases. In adjudication, bureaucrats must decide whether an individual, firm, or corpo-ration has complied with laws and regulations and, if not, what penalties or correc-tive actions are to be imposed. Formal bureaucratic adjudication resembles the judicial process, while bureaucratic regulation resembles the legislative process. Federal regulatory agencies—for example, the Environmental Protection Agency, the Equal Employment Opportunity Commission, the Federal Trade Commis-sion, the Securities and Exchange Commission—as well as the Internal Revenue Service, are heavily engaged in adjudication. These bureaucracies have established procedures for investigation, notification, hearing, decision, and appeal. Bureau-cratic adjudication is somewhat less formal than a court trial, "defendants" have fewer procedural rights, and the "judges" are employees of the agency itself. The record of agency decisions in individual cases, for example, decisions by the Inter-nal Revenue Service about what are or are not lawful deductions, become in effect public policy. In other words, just as previous court decisions reflect judicial policy, previous administrative decisions reflect bureaucratic policy.

Bureaucrats may also exercise considerable discretion in much of their "routine" work. Bureaucratic discretion may extend to such seemingly routine administrative tasks as determining Social Security eligibility, approving Medicare claims, granting veterans' benefits, issuing broadcast licenses, and so on. Often individual cases do not exactly fit established regulations; often more than one regulation might be applied to the same case, resulting in different outcomes. For example, the Internal Revenue Service has developed hundreds of thousands of rules interpreting the U.S. Tax Code, but each IRS office has wide discretion in deciding which rules to apply to an individual taxpayer's income, deductions, business expenses, and so on. Indeed, identical tax information submitted to different IRS offices almost always results in different estimates of tax liability. But even in the performance of the most routine tasks, bureaucrats can be friendly and helpful or hostile and obstructive.

Individuals, firms, and corporations are at a considerable disadvantage in confronting a federal bureaucracy. Federal bureaucracies, especially regulatory agencies, have armies of attorneys, paid for out of tax monies, to defend themselves in court. It is very expensive for individual systems to challenge agency actions. Corporations and interest groups must weigh the cost of litigation against the cost of compliance before undertaking a legal challenge to a bureaucratic decision. Appeals of bureaucratic decisions to the courts are usually unsuccessful.[9] Federal courts step in *only* when a bureaucratic action violates laws of Congress, or when an action exceeds the authority granted the bureaucracies under law, or when the bureaucracy's action has been judged "arbitrary and unreasonable," or when a bureaucracy fails in its legal duties under the law. Federal courts will also step in when the bureaucracy has failed to follow procedural guidelines—for example, proper notice, fair hearing, right of appeal, and so on. In short, judicial oversight tends to focus only on (1) whether or not agencies are acting beyond the authority granted to them by Congress; and (2) whether or not they are abiding by the procedural rules. The courts generally do *not* review the *policy* decisions of the bureaucracy. If policy decisions are made under the legal authority granted to the bureaucracy by Congress, and if they have been made in a procedurally correct fashion, courts generally do not intervene.

CHAPTER 9

The Policy Evaluation Process

*Wilson's First Law: All policy interventions in social problems produce the
intended effect—if the research is carried out by those implementing the
policy or by their friends.*

*Wilson's Second Law: No policy intervention in social problems produces
the intended effect—if the research is carried out by independent third
parties, especially those skeptical of the policy.*

—JAMES Q. WILSON

POLICY EVALUATION IS learning about the effects, if any, of public policy, and
trying to determine whether these effects are what was intended, and whether
the effects are worth the costs of the policy. Americans often assume that if
Congress passes a law and appropriates money for a particular purpose, and if
the executive branch organizes a program and spends money to carry out the
activities mandated by the law, then the effects of the law will be felt by society
and will be those intended by Congress. But this seldom turns out to be the case.

DEFINING POLICY EVALUATION

According to the Government Accounting Office (GAO), "Program evaluation—
when it is available and of high-quality—provides sound information about what
programs are actually delivering, how they are being managed, and the extent to
which they are cost-effective."[1] Similar definitions of policy (program) evaluation are
found in the literature in public administration. Most of these definitions include
references to "objectives" or "goals" of policies, their "effects" or "impact" on "target"
groups and populations, and their "costs."[2] It sounds simple, but it is not.

Specifying Objectives

Policy evaluation is a very complex process. It involves, first, the specification of goals
and objectives, that is, desired outcomes, of government programs. But the stated
goals of programs are often ambiguously expressed, sometimes deliberately so by a
Congress seeking to satisfy multiple interests simultaneously. We do not always

know what the goals of government programs really are, and it is not uncommon for government programs to pursue multiple and even conflicting goals.

Developing Measures

Second, policy evaluation requires the development of measures of the impact of government activities. Measuring policy *impact* is not the same as measuring policy *output*; that is, it is not the same as measuring how much money is spent by government agencies or how many "clients" are served. Rather, policy evaluation requires the measurement of actual changes in society brought about by the policy. Governments produce reams of statistics about, for example, Social Security beneficiaries, welfare recipients, public school pupils, crimes reported to police, and prisoners in correctional institutions, as well as the money it spends on its programs. But this "bean counting" tells us very little about the financial condition of the aged, the extent or hardship of poverty, the reading or analytic skills of children, or the safety of the American public. We cannot know how far a bird flies by counting how many times it flaps its wings.

Identifying Target Groups

Moreover, policy evaluation requires an assessment of the impact of government activities on both "target" groups (those whom the policies are intended to affect) as well as "nontarget" groups (others whom the policies may affect).[3] For example, even if property seizures were shown to reduce drug trafficking, what is the impact of these seizures on innocent citizens or on American civil liberties generally? Policy evaluation should include both intended and *unintended* consequences, and both short-term and long-term effects. Many policy studies show that new or innovative programs have a short-term positive effect; but often positive effects disappear as the novelty and enthusiasm for a new program wears off.

Measuring Costs

Policy evaluation also requires estimates of the true costs of a policy, in both dollar and nondollar terms. This means not only accurately reporting the cost of a program in the government's budget, but also determining whether a policy incurs costs to society that are not reflected in the government spending. Often the costs of policies are deliberately hidden by decision makers and the benefits overstated. In regulatory policy especially, costs are deliberately shifted from government to the private sector. Such shifting of costs makes evaluation particularly difficult; indeed, making evaluation difficult may be one of the objectives of the policy.

Evaluating Costs and Benefits

Finally, and perhaps most important, policy evaluation requires a calculation of the *net balance* of the benefits and costs of a policy or program. Even if all of the costs and benefits are known and measurable (and everyone agrees on what is a "benefit" or a "cost"), calculating the net balance is still very difficult. Do the benefits exceed the costs, or vice versa? Many benefits (e.g., saving lives) and costs (e.g., lost liberties) cannot be translated into dollars, and it therefore frequently is impossible to make cost-benefit calculations. Nonetheless, policies *are* evaluated, although seldom in a truly systematic fashion. Elites are made aware through a variety of ways of how well or how badly government programs are performing.

TOP-DOWN POLICY EVALUATION

Top-down policy evaluation occurs as elites try to discern whether current policies correspond to their own preferences, interests, and values. Elites may receive "feedback" regarding the effects of government policies in a variety of ways (see figure 9.1). They may directly discern policy effects themselves from the information they receive through the institutions they themselves direct—corporations, banks, insurance companies, investment firms, media conglomerates. Reports about the effects of government policies regularly filter up from "the field." These reports link government policies to the operations of the institutions, including their "bottom line," that is, their profits.

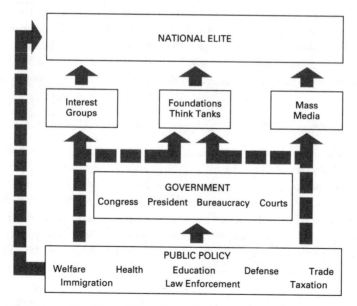

Figure 9.1 Top-Down Policy Evaluation

Note: Broken lines indicate "feedback" linkages.

Elites are also kept appraised of the effect of government policies by interest groups. Much of the daily work of interest groups in Washington consists of monitoring the operations of government agencies in order to protect the interests of sponsoring elites. Indeed, interest groups generally exercise even closer oversight of bureaucracies than do the president and White House or Congress and its committees. Interest groups can specialize in monitoring the effects of agency programs, regulations, expenditures, and activities on the particular interests of their sponsors. To keep tabs on public policies and their effects on their clients' interests, organized groups in Washington generally seek to maintain close relationships with both the congressional committees with jurisdiction over their policy field and the executive agencies charged with implementing these policies. The result is the familiar "iron triangle" of stable relationships between interest groups, congressional committees, and bureaucratic agencies functioning in the same policy arena. Yet another familiar result is the development of "policy networks"—regular friendly interactions between people working in interest group offices, congressional committee offices, and government agencies.

Foundations and think tanks also play an important role in top-down policy evaluation. These institutions, already described as central to the *formulation* of policy, also regularly undertake the *evaluation* of current policies. Indeed, policy formulation and policy evaluation are closely related: foundation-funded studies by think tanks often assess the effects of current policies.

The mass media regularly engage in their own form of policy evaluation, usually stories about corruption, scandal, and mismanagement in government, as well as stories about the ill-effects of government programs (see feature: "What the Mass Public Thinks about Government Waste," pp. 162–63). Watchdog reporting (see "The Politics of the Media" in chapter 6) is designed to spotlight evil in high places, waste and fraud in government, and wrongdoing in Washington. While elites may disregard much of the "hype" that accompanies such stories, they cannot ignore them altogether. Media stories frequently set the agenda for conversations among elites, especially when stories are carried by the *New York Times, Washington Post,* or *Wall Street Journal,* or by the major television networks. These stories often inspire elites to undertake their own review of the policies and programs under fire in the media.

Government itself seldom undertakes meaningful policy evaluation. Government agencies, of course, regularly hold hearings, undertake program reviews, issue reports, and produce volumes of statistics regarding their programs. Governments frequently report on policy *outputs,* but they seldom undertake to measure the *impacts* of their activities on society. Nor do they undertake to calculate the ratio of benefits to costs, even when they are occasionally mandated by Congress to do so (see discussion later in this chapter). Bureaucrats often look with suspicion on efforts to evaluate their programs. They perceive policy evaluation as a potential threat to their organization, its functions and authority, and their own power and position.

FEATURE: WHAT THE MASS PUBLIC THINKS ABOUT GOVERNMENT WASTE

The mass public equates bureaucracy with red tape, paper shuffling, dupli-
cation of effort, impersonality, senseless regulation, and unresponsiveness
to the needs of ordinary people. And it equates government bureaucracy
with waste and inefficiency.

Indeed, over the years an overwhelming majority of Americans have
remained convinced that government "wastes *a lot* of the money we pay in
taxes," not just "some," or "not very much."

*Q: Do people in the government waste a lot of the money we pay in taxes, some of
it, or not very much of it?*

	1998	1996	1988	1984
A lot	65	63	64	65
Some	32	33	34	29
Not very much	3	4	3	4

Source: National Election Studies.

Are Americans correct in their judgment that government wastes "a
lot" of money? Over the years the General Accounting Office audits have
frequently found fraud and mismanagement amounting to around 10
percent of the spending of many government agencies.[a] These studies have
given rise to a general estimate that the federal government wastes about
$170 *billion* a year out of its overall budget of about $1.7 trillion. But citizens' commissions studying the federal bureaucracy frequently place a
higher figure on waste. The Grace Commission in 1984 estimated federal
government waste at more than 20 percent of federal spending.[b]

Elites are not unaware of the public's view of the federal bureaucracy;
virtually every presidential administration has promised to end waste and
inefficiency. The current notion of "reinventing government" gained popularity among centrist Democrats even before the Clinton administration
arrived in Washington. Not all Democratic Party constituencies—notably
government employees and their unions, teachers and their unions, and
environmental groups—are enthusiastic about the antibureaucratic thrust
of the "reinventing government" movement.[c] But upon taking office, Clinton assigned the task to Al Gore. The vice president promptly produced the
168-page National Performance Review, *Creating a Government That Works
Better and Costs Less,* with 384 specific recommendations designed to put
the "customer" (citizen) first, to "empower" federal bureaucrats to get
things done, to introduce competition in public services, and to decentral-

ize government decision making.[d] Regular "reinventing" reports that have been issued from Gore's office boast of better governmental services at lower cost.[e] But even after discounting for puffery, some progress appears to have been achieved. The most impressive evidence is an overall decline of about 200,000 federal government employees (about 7 percent of the federal civilian workforce).

a. General Accounting Office, *Federal Evaluation Issues* (Washington, D.C.: GAO, 1989).
b. *President's Private Sector Survey on Cost Control*, GAO Commission Report (Washington, D.C.: Government Printing Office, 1984).
c. David Osborne and Ted Gaebler, *Reinventing Government: How the Entrepreneurial Spirit Is Transforming the Public Sector* (New York: Addison-Wesley, 1992), 23–24.
d. Al Gore, *Creating a Government That Works Better and Costs Less* (Washington, D.C.: Government Printing Office, 1993).
e. Al Gore, *The Best Kept Secrets in Washington: How the Clinton Administration Is Reinventing the Way Government Works* (New York: Random House, 1996).

POLICY EVALUATION BY GOVERNMENTS

Governments occasionally attempt to evaluate the effects of their own policies. Indeed, in recent years, "program evaluation" has become a common buzzword in bureaucratic circles. But governments seldom produce meaningful policy evaluations.

A concerted effort to assess the costs and benefits of regulatory activity was initiated by President Ronald Reagan, who, by presidential order, required executive agencies to submit all *new* regulations for review by the Office of Management and Budget (OMB) to ensure that the economic costs imposed by these regulations were justified by the expected benefits. In 1995 the Republican Congress mandated that the OMB submit to Congress an economic assessment of each new regulation. But the OMB under Democratic president Bill Clinton has been much more favorably disposed toward regulation, especially by the Environmental Protection Agency, the Federal Trade Commission, and the Food and Drug Administration. The result has been that the economic cost assessments of proposed new regulations have become largely a meaningless procedural exercise.

Perhaps in recognition of popular discontent with waste and inefficiency in government, in 1993 Congress passed the largely symbolic Government Performance and Results Act. The stated purpose of the act was to make federal programs justify their existence on the basis of positive changes they brought about in society. Federal agencies are now supposed to monitor the effects of their activities on their client groups, but "the danger, as with many other exercises in evaluation, is that Congress will focus attention on a few quantitative indicators and fail to understand the complexity of both evaluation and the programs that are being evaluated."[4]

Government program reviews are generally limited to the following:

- *Hearings and reports.* Executive agencies, as well as Congress itself, regularly hold hearings and require reports on the activities and accomplishments of programs. OMB and relevant congressional committees listen to the testimony of program officials and frequently require them to provide written annual reports on their agencies' activities. But these testimonials and reports usually magnify the benefits and minimize the costs of the program, and they seldom provide objective policy evaluations.

- *Programmatic output measures.* The reports of government agencies themselves are usually limited to data on policy outputs, for example, the number of recipients in various welfare programs, the number of persons participating in work training programs, the number of pupils enrolled in schools. But these reports do not include much evaluative information, for example, whether welfare recipients eventually overcome poverty, whether work trainees ever find jobs in the occupations for which they trained, and whether pupils are actually learning reading, writing, and arithmetic. (In recent years, though, the debate over educational quality in America has focused greater attention on measures of achievement.)

- *Citizens' complaints and opinions.* Many government agencies are increasingly using telephone hot-lines to gather information regarding various kinds of citizen complaints. And, of course, members of Congress frequently receive calls and letters from constituents complaining about the activities of federal bureaucracies. But seldom there is any way to judge whether these complaints arise from only a vocal few or are shared by many more who have not spoken up. Occasionally, government agencies will develop questionnaires for their clients, or for citizens generally, asking whether they are satisfied with current levels of service. But such polls usually produce favorable results; citizens, especially client groups of government agencies, usually favor the continuation or even the expansion of government services. These questionnaires seldom focus on costs, and popular opinion about programs is not the equivalent of systematic program evaluation.

The Government Accounting Office regularly conducts somewhat more useful studies of federal programs. The GAO was established in the same Budget and Accounting Act of 1921 that created the first executive budget. (Thus, the GAO was yet another policy innovation attributable to the Brookings Institution.) Initially, GAO confined itself to financial auditing of government programs, but in the Congressional Budget and Impoundment Act of 1974, it was given increased authority to undertake evaluative studies. The GAO is actually an arm of Congress, rather than an executive branch agency, so its reports go directly to Congress. The GAO regularly laments the absence of meaningful program evaluation in federal executive agencies. Over the years, GAO studies have been especially critical of the Defense Department for failing to test weapons systems adequately before authorizing production and for failure to monitor defense industry contractors and their charges. Most GAO reports are requested by Congress, but the office is authorized to undertake evaluative studies on its own initiative.

Why does government usually fail in its own efforts at program evaluation? First, government agencies have a strong vested interest in showing that their programs have a positive impact. Bureaucrats frequently view attempts to evaluate their programs by outside, independent organizations as threats to their program, its budget, or their own competence as administrators. Government agencies are unlikely to produce studies showing that their programs do not work or that their costs exceed their benefits. Second, program evaluation requires the allocation of funds, facilities, and personnel, which agencies do not like to sacrifice. Bureaucrats must give priority to the conduct of day-to-day business over study and evaluation. Finally, bureaucrats understand that their programs often have more symbolic and political value than actual substantive impact on society. They know, as do members of Congress, that many policies do not actually change the conditions of target groups but merely make these groups feel that government cares. Government agencies do not welcome studies that reveal that their activities have little tangible effect; such results may even reduce the symbolic and political value of programs by revealing their ineffectiveness.

THE CONTINUATION OF FAILED PROGRAMS

Government programs are rarely terminated—they manage to survive even when evaluative studies produce negative findings; even when members of Congress are well aware of these studies; even when highly negative benefit-cost ratios are widely reported. Policies, programs, and organizations are very sturdy. Usually the worst fate they ever suffer is a reduction in their budgets.

Why do policies and programs persist long after their ineffectiveness has been demonstrated? One reason for the continuation of ineffective government programs and policies is that their limited benefits are concentrated on small, well-organized constituencies, while their greater costs are dispersed over a large, unorganized, uninformed public. Although few in number, beneficiaries of a program are usually strongly committed to it and active in their support of it. If the costs of the program are spread widely among all taxpayers, buried in a multitrillion-dollar budget, then no one has a strong incentive to become organized or active in opposition to it. The mass public's general discontent with the waste, inefficiency, and costs of government seldom provides sufficient incentive for policymakers to overcome the support of special interest groups for their favorite programs.

Moreover, among the principal beneficiaries of any government program are the bureaucrats who administer it and the members of congressional committees that oversee it. Bureaucrats whose benefits, pay, authority, and prestige are at stake have a natural tendency to attack negative evaluations of their programs, or to respond to criticism by making only marginal changes in policy, or even to claim that if their programs are failing it is because *not enough* money is being spent on them. In Congress the committee system, with its investment of authority over programs to members most friendly to them, invites "logrolling" ("You support my committee's program and I'll support yours"). Legislators on committees with jurisdiction over a program are usually the largest recipients of campaign contributions from the organized beneficiaries of that program. These legislators can use their committee positions to protect failed programs, to minimize reforms, and to block efforts at termination.

In addition, the incremental nature of most policymaking limits active consideration of policies and programs to their margins—that is, attention is focused on proposed changes in existing programs and their budgets rather than on the value of existing programs in their entirety. Negative evaluative studies can play a role in the budgetary process, limiting increases for failed programs and perhaps even identifying programs ripe for budget cutting. But incrementalism almost always focuses attention on changes or reforms, increases or decreases, rather than on the complete termination of programs.

Finally, failed programs can always be "reformed" or "repackaged"—slightly modified, or given new names and agency titles, while maintaining essentially the same bureaucracies and the same policy prescriptions. For example, many of the programs of President Lyndon Johnson's War on Poverty in the 1960s were repackaged and placed in different departments following the official termination of the Office of Economic Opportunity. The failed job program under the Comprehensive Employment and Training Act (CETA) was repackaged in the 1970s by Senators Edward Kennedy and Dan Quayle as the Job Training and Placement Service (JTPS) program, with only modest reforms and continuing reports of few benefits and excessive costs. Government bureaucracies themselves may generate "reforms" when they face possible reductions in their authority or budgets imposed from the outside. Prudent bureaucrats and legislators seeking to rescue failed programs often initiate reforms themselves and convince their client groups to agree to them rather than risk reductions or termination. (See feature: "How to Explain Away Failed Policies.")

POLICY EVALUATION BY ELITES

Policy change occurs when elites determine that policies are failing to serve their interests and values or could be better designed to do so. Policy change is a less traumatic and a more frequent occurrence than policy formulation—the development of completely new policy directions, programs, and organizations.

Policy change resembles the same top-down process described for policy

FEATURE: HOW TO EXPLAIN AWAY FAILED POLICIES

Bureaucrats and program supporters are ingenious in devising reasons why failed policies should be continued. Despite clear evidence of the failure of policies or programs, they will argue:

- The effects of the policy are intended to be long-range and cannot be measured at the present time.
- The program is designed to produce qualitative changes that cannot be identified by crude statistical measures.
- The program is intended produce multiple effects; no single measure or index can adequately assess the success of the program.
- The failure of the program to produce any positive effects means that the program is not sufficiently intensive and indicates a need to spend *more* resources on the program.

The failure of an evaluative study to show positive results of a program is claimed to be a product of a poor research design, or worse, a product of a negative bias on the part of the people or the organization conducting the study.

Bureaucrats prefer to carry out their own evaluations of their programs or to oversee contracts for studies by consulting firms that the bureaucrats themselves choose. They prefer to use a short time-frame (a long time-frame maximizes the likelihood of observing negative outcomes or failure). Of course, evaluations undertaken by individuals or organizations politically hostile to the policy are likely to adopt a short time-frame that minimizes the likelihood of observing positive effects, or if they are observed, allows them to argue that the results are temporary or a product of the Hawthorne effect (the reaction of people to the fact that they are part of an experiment), and that maximizes the search for factors other than the policy itself that might explain positive effects.

formulation (see chapter 3). In contrast to major policy initiatives, however, policy changes do not involve the discovery of new unaddressed threats to elite values or any substantial revision of elite goals or objectives. Rather, policy changes usually involve modest adjustments of existing policies—"policy reform"—or the replacement of existing programs with new programs designed to accomplish the same goals—"policy succession."[5] Neither policy reform nor policy succession requires the same elite involvement as the formulation of totally new government policies. Neither requires the redefinition or revision of elite values or goals.

Policy "entrepreneurship" by officeholders and office seekers is a major stimulus to policy change. Politicians at every level of government, including presidents, members of Congress, and candidates for these offices, regularly engage in policy "entrepreneurship"—advocating specific policy changes as a means of self-promotion. Generally policy entrepreneurship is limited to proposals to improve on existing policies and program, that is, to better accomplish established goals or to do so at a lower cost. (Politicians who choose to advocate radical change or the replacement of established elite values are subject to the discipline of the leadership selection process. See chapter 5.) Elites are often satisfied to allow politicians, bureaucrats, and interest groups to try to improve on legislation designed to accomplish previously agreed-on goals.

Agenda setting is not as difficult for policy reform or succession as it is for policy innovation. The initial "problem"—the condition in society deemed undesirable—has already been identified. All that needs to be done is to convince decision makers that current policies or programs are inadequate and should be improved on or replaced. Returning an issue to the policy agenda is more easily accomplished than initially introducing it.

Interest groups play a major role in monitoring the policies and programs that directly affect their sponsoring elites. Interest groups try to maintain close working relationships with the government agencies that serve their members or regulate their industries. At the same time, they also try to maintain close relationships with the standing congressional committees and subcommittees that have "oversight" of these agencies, and with the Appropriations subcommittees that handle their budgets. Bureaucrats often seek to nourish close ties with interest groups in order to gain leverage with Congress to expand their authority and increase their budgets. And, of course, members of Congress are especially dependent on campaign contributions from the interest groups over which their committees have authority. The mutual interests of congressional committee members, the government agencies that they oversee, and the "client" interest groups that they serve come together to form what have been labeled the "iron triangles" of American government.

Of course conflict, rather than cooperation, characterizes some bureaucratic–congressional–interest group relationships. Conflict is more likely to occur in those agencies given comprehensive authority over the environment, or safety and health, or advertising, or race relations, rather than specialized authority over a particular industry. Thus, the Environmental Protection Agency, which is dependent on the environmental movement for its existence, frequently comes into conflict with industry. The Occupational Safety and Health Administration is often caught between the demands of big labor unions and industry groups. The Federal Trade Commission depends heavily on the support of consumer organizations, and it, too, frequently comes in conflict with industry.

But even in these seemingly conflictual policy areas, it is not uncommon for "policy networks" to develop—regular interactions and personal relationships between interest group leaders, lobbyists, members of Congress and their staff, government officials in executive agencies, lawyers and consultants, and foundation and think tank personnel, who all work in the same policy area. Policy networks may include people who differ from one another as well as those who share similar views. What they have in common is their policy expertise, for example, in housing, transportation, energy, or environmental affairs, and their regular personal interaction with one another.

Policy networks facilitate the development of "revolving doors"—the movement of people in a policy network from one job to another in that policy field. For example, an individual might move from a job in a corporation (Pillsbury or General Mills) to the staff of an interest group (American Farm Bureau Federation), and then to the executive agency charged with implementing policy in the field (U.S. Department of Agriculture) or to the House or Senate committee with jurisdiction over the field (House Agriculture Committee or Senate Agriculture, Nutrition, and Forestry Committee). Often the term "revolving doors" is used critically to label those people who move from a government post to a job in the private sector as a lobbyist, consultant, lawyer, or salesperson for a government contractor, where they can cash in on the knowledge, experience, and contacts they acquired in their government job at taxpayers' expense. For example, congressional staffers, White House staffers, or high-ranking agency officials may be recruited by business or trade associations to become lobbyists; or attorneys from the Justice Department, the Internal Revenue Service, or other federal regulatory agencies may be recruited by Washington law firms to represent big-money clients in dealings with their former employers. Indeed, following retirement, many members of Congress have turned to lobbying their former colleagues (including former Senate majority leaders Democrat George Mitchell and Republican Bob Dole; see chapter 5).

But policy networks and revolving doors also raise the possibility of government bureaucrats and members of Congress tilting their decisions in favor of corporations, law firms, and interest groups, with the expectation that at some point in the future they may be seeking employment from them. The Ethics in Government Act (an oxymoron?) prohibits former members of Congress from lobbying Congress for one year after leaving that body, and it prohibits bureaucrats from lobbying their own agency for two years on any matter over which they had any responsibility while employed by that agency. But of course the law does not prohibit "opening doors" or "schmoozing" or simply maintaining friendly relationships.

Foundations and think tanks play a crucial role in policy change—both in policy reform and in policy succession. A review of the publications of influential think tanks indicates that at least as much work goes into policy evaluation and recommendations for reform as into the origination of new policies (see table 9.1, p. 170). For example, the Brookings Institution has published a number of influential books and articles on the reform of the Social Security system, and it is deeply involved in current efforts to maintain and expand the Medicare and

Table 9.1   Selected Policy Evaluation Studies by Leading Think Tanks

COUNCIL ON FOREIGN RELATIONS

- *U.S. Policy toward North Korea: A Second Look*
- *Reconstructing the Balkans*
- *U.S.–Cuban Relations in the 21st Century*
- *Strengthening Palestinian Institutions*
- *National Minorities and Conflict in Eastern Europe*

BROOKINGS INSTITUTION

- *The Case against Tax Cuts*
- *Restructuring Social Security Taxes*
- *Privatizing Social Security: The Troubling Trade-offs*
- *Environmental Policy: The Next Generation*
- *Teen Pregnancy Prevention: Welfare Reform's Missing Component*
- *You Can't Get There from Here: Government Failure in U.S. Transportation*
- *Medicaid and Devolution*

HERITAGE FOUNDATION

- *The Impact of Welfare Reform: The Trend in State Case Loads*
- *No Excuses: Seven Principals of Low Income Schools Who Set Standards for High Achievement*
- *The IRS v. The People*
- *School Choice Helps Public Schools*
- *America at Risk: The Citizens' Guide to Missile Defense*

AMERICAN ENTERPRISE INSTITUTE

- *Good Intentions: The Failure of the Clinton Approach to Foreign Policy*
- *The Frayed Social Contract: Why Social Security Is in Trouble*
- *The Effects of the Minimum Wage on Employment*
- *Using Federalism to Improve Environmental Policy*
- *Restoring Consumer Sovereignty to Products Liability*

Note: Titles of selected policy evaluation studies, 1996–99.

Medicaid programs. The more conservative Heritage Foundation has also devoted efforts to reforming Social Security, urging that individuals be allowed to invest their Social Security savings in the stock market. And welfare reform was a major topic of think tank work in the years leading up to the Welfare Reform Act of 1996 (see feature: "Evaluation and Reform of Welfare Policy").

POLITICS AND POLICY EVALUATION

Policy evaluation is a *political* process. It can proceed along a fairly rational course when elites agree on societal goals, when they agree on what problems the government should undertake to resolve, when they agree on the nature of societal benefits and costs and the weights to be given to them. But broad agreement

FEATURE: EVALUATION AND REFORM OF WELFARE POLICY

The most comprehensive reform of federal policy in recent years is the Welfare Reform Act of 1996. It ended the sixty-year-old federal cash entitlement program for low-income families with children. It replaced the program of direct federal family entitlements to cash assistance enacted in 1935—Aid to Families with Dependent Children (AFDC)—with a federal grant program to the states that allocates money to fund their own family cash assistance programs—Temporary Assistance to Needy Families (TANF). The act represented a "devolution" of responsibility for welfare cash aid from the federal government to the states. It was the first major revision of federal welfare policy and the first transfer of a major federal program from Washington to the states.

How did welfare reform come about? Throughout the 1970s and 1980s, federal welfare and antipoverty programs were the subject of a large number of evaluative studies. But perhaps the most influential of these studies was Charles Murray's *Losing Ground,* published in 1984. Murray's work was *not* funded by the federal government, but rather by the New York–based think tank, the Manhattan Institute.

Murray argued in *Losing Ground* that federal welfare programs were themselves contributing to poverty by destroying incentives to work, encouraging families to break up, and condemning the poor to social dependency. The social welfare system, Murray contended, unintentionally sentenced to a life of poverty many people who would otherwise form families, accept low-paying jobs, and perhaps, with hard work, gradually pull themselves and their children into mainstream American life.

Murray assembled statistics showing that poverty in America had steadily *declined* from 1950, when about 30 percent of the population was officially poor, to 1970, when about 13 percent of the population was poor. Welfare rolls were modest during this time: only about 1 to 2 percent of Americans received AFDC payments. But the downward trend in poverty ended with the addition of many new Great Society welfare programs in the 1960s and a subsequent growth in welfare rolls to about 5 to 6 percent of the population. The Food Stamp program was initiated in 1965 and became a major new welfare benefit. Medicaid was initiated in the same year and by the late 1970s became the costliest welfare program. The Supplemental Security Income program (SSI) replaced more modest federal aid programs to the aged, blind, and disabled, and it quadrupled the number of "disabled" recipients. The number of people living below the poverty line rose from 25 million to nearly 40 million, and the percentage of the population living in poverty stopped declining and remained between 13 and 15 percent.

Murray argued that the expansion of the welfare state was actually hurting, not helping, the poor. He argued that generous welfare programs encouraged poor young women to start families before they had sufficient job skills to support them, and that they allowed poor young men to escape their family responsibilities. Long-term reliance on welfare payments created a dependent and defeatist subculture, lowering personal self-esteem and contributing further to joblessness, illegitimacy, and broken families.

Murray's policy prescription was a drastic one. He recommended "scrapping the entire federal welfare and income-support system for working-age persons. It would leave the working-age person with no recourse whatever except the job market, family members, friends, and public or private locally funded services . . . cut the knot, for there is no way to untie it." The result, he argued, would be less poverty, less illegitimacy, more upward mobility, and greater hope for the poor.

Although Murray's work was bitterly condemned by liberals, it forced elites to reconsider a variety of problems in social welfare policy: the work disincentives created by the pyramiding of multiple forms of public assistance, the long-term social dependency that welfare programs seemed to encourage, and the adverse effects welfare assistance appeared to have on families. (Poverty is most common among female-headed families; almost 40 percent of such families live below the poverty line, compared to only about 6 percent of married couples.) Liberals and conservatives joined together to pass a Family Support Act of 1988 intended to reform AFDC by requiring that states offer federally assisted job training "workfare" programs to adults receiving AFDC cash assistance. But welfare rolls continued to rise in the early 1990s, expanding from 10 million persons to nearly 15 million.

After a great deal of controversy and two presidential vetoes, welfare reform finally became law in 1996. It was passed by a Republican-controlled Congress and signed by a Democratic president during an election year, but it was bitterly opposed by social workers, minorities, and many liberal Democrats. The AFDC federal cash assistance entitlement program was ended, and it was succeeded by TANF federal block grants to the states. TANF reflected the philosophy of devolution of responsibility to the states; the states were given greater authority to determine benefits and eligibility requirements for cash assistance.

But Murray's arguments were also reflected in the act. Various tough-minded "strings" were attached to federal aid, including a two-year limit on continuing cash benefits and a five-year lifetime limit; a "family cap" that denies additional cash benefits to women already on welfare who bear more children; the denial of cash welfare to unwed mothers under eighteen years of age unless they live with an adult and attend school. Liberals in Congress managed to insert a few modifying provisions, including exemptions from time limits for some portion of welfare recipients and community service alternatives to work requirements.

Welfare reform itself is now the subject of policy evaluation. Many early critics, as well as supporters, of welfare reform have come to view it as a success. This evaluation is based primarily on the rapid decline in the nation's welfare rolls over the past several years (see figure 9A). The number of welfare recipients in the nation has now dropped below 10 million—the lowest number in more than twenty-five years and the smallest proportion of the population (4 percent) since 1970. No doubt some of this decline is attributable to strong growth in the economy: declines in welfare rolls actually began *before* Congress passed welfare reform. But virtually all of the states have substantially reduced their welfare rolls. Applicants for welfare benefits are now generally required to enter job-search programs, to undertake job training, or to accept jobs or community service positions when offered, or they will be denied cash assistance.

But it is not yet clear whether persons who have been dropped from welfare rolls or have been denied application for assistance have suffered undue hardships. Moreover, a substantial portion (perhaps 25 to 40

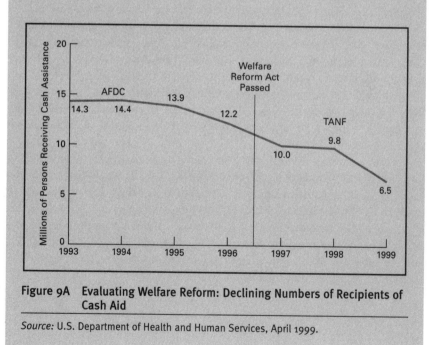

Figure 9A Evaluating Welfare Reform: Declining Numbers of Recipients of Cash Aid

Source: U.S. Department of Health and Human Services, April 1999.

percent) of long-term welfare recipients have handicaps—physical disabilities, chronic illnesses, alcohol or drug abuse problems—that prevent them from holding a job. More than half of these long-term recipients did not graduate from high school, and almost half have three or more children, making day-care arrangements a necessity. Even if there are 5 million jobs available to unskilled mothers, most are low-paying and may not lift these women or their children out of poverty.

Note: Quotations are from Charles Murray, *Losing Ground* (New York: Basic Books, 1984).

on societal goals and the role of government does not ensure the absence of conflict about the appropriate *means* of achieving these goals or the appropriate role of government in doing so. Such conflict can invade virtually every aspect of policy evaluation—the appropriate design of research, the measurement of specific benefits and costs and the weight to be given to them, and the interpretation of results. In policy evaluation, "there is never a point at which the thinking, research, and action is 'objective' or 'unbiased.' It is partisan through and through, as are all human activities, in the sense that the expectations and priorities of those commissioning and doing the analysis shape it, and in the sense that those using the information shape its interpretation and application."[6]

The top-down models of policy evaluation and formulation do not suggest that elites never disagree about public policy. Elites may share a consensus about goals and values yet disagree on how to achieve them. And it is unlikely that there ever was a society in which elites did not compete among themselves for power and preeminence. But disagreements and competition among elites take place within a shared consensus about the importance of economic growth, private property, and limited government. Disagreement occurs over the *means* rather than the *ends* of public policy.

It is the shared consensus among elites over the fundamental values of American society that allows public policy to be guided by "the intelligence of democracy." Political scientist Charles E. Lindblom explains the intelligence of democracy: "Strategic analysis and mutual adjustment among political participants, then, are the underlying processes by which democratic systems achieve the level of intelligent action that they do."[7] But strategic analysis and mutual adjustment—the keys to intelligent policymaking—cannot develop in the absence of agreement on fundamental values.

Notes

NOTES TO CHAPTER 1

1. E.E. Schattschneider, *Two Hundred Million Americans in Search of a Government* (New York: Holt, Rinehart & Winston, 1969), 63.
2. Charles E. Lindblom and Edward J. Woodhouse, *The Policymaking Process*, 3d ed. (Englewood Cliffs, N.J.: Prentice Hall, 1993), 9.
3. See Thomas R. Dye, *Understanding Public Policy*, 9th ed. (Upper Saddle River, N.J.: Prentice Hall, 1998), 2–4.
4. C. Wright Mills, *The Power Elite* (New York: Oxford University Press, 1956), 9.
5. For various descriptions of America's elite, see G. William Domhoff, *Who Rules America? Power and Politics in the Year 2000* (Mountain View, Calif.: Mayfield, 1998); Thomas R. Dye, *Who's Running America?* 6th ed. (Englewood Cliffs, N.J.: Prentice Hall, 1995); and Robert Lerner, Althea K. Nagai, and Stanley Rothman, *American Elites* (New Haven: Yale University Press, 1996).
6. For an argument that the relative autonomy of elite groups is necessary for the preservation of democracy, see Eva Etzioni-Halevy, *The Elite Connection* (Cambridge, Mass.: Polity Press, 1993).

NOTES TO CHAPTER 2

1. James Madison, *Federalist* No. 10.
2. *Fortune*, 27 April 1999, 138.
3. U.S. Bureau of the Census, *Statistical Abstract of the United States, 1998*.
4. *Statistical Abstract of the United States, 1999*, 478.
5. *Statistical Abstract of the United States, 1999*, 417.
6. Regional Financial Associates, as reported in *U.S. News & World Report*, 1 November, 1999.
7. Edward N. Wolff, *Top Heavy: A Study of Increasing Inequality of Wealth in America* (New York: Twentieth Century Fund, 1995).
8. Ibid.
9. Richard B. Freeman, "Are Your Wages Set in Beijing?" *Journal of Economic Perspectives* 9 (Summer 1995): 15.
10. Madison, *Federalist* No. 10.
11. Quoted in Richard Hofstadter, *The American Political Tradition* (New York: Knopf, 1948), 45.
12. See Herbert McClosky and John Zaller, *The American Ethos* (Cambridge, Mass.: Harvard University Press, 1984).
13. See James R. Kluegel and Eliot R. Smith, *Beliefs about Inequality* (New York: Aldine, 1986).
14. Gallup International Research, as reported in *U.S. News & World Report*, 7 August 1989.
15. Council of Economic Advisers, *Economic Report of the President, 1995* (Washington, D.C.: Government Printing Office, 1995), 232.

NOTES TO CHAPTER 3

1. G. William Domhoff, *Who Rules America? Power and Politics in the Year 2000* (Mountain View, Calif.: Mayfield, 1998), 127.
2. *The Foundation Directory 1999* (New York: The Foundation Center, 1999).
3. Quoted in *Forbes*, 15 May 1972.
4. Carnegie Corporation of New York, *Mission Statement*, 1999.
5. Leonard Silk and Mark Silk, *The American Establishment* (New York: Basic Books, 1980), 160.
6. Brookings also served as chairman of the board of trustees of Washington University in St. Louis for twenty years, building a small college into a major university.
7. Quoting AEI President William Baroody Jr. in Silk and Silk, *American Establishment*, 179.
8. Heritage Foundation, *Annual Report 1985*, 1.
9. Heritage Foundation, *Mission Statement*, 1999.
10. Council on Foreign Relations, *Annual Report, 1979–80*, 11.
11. Council on Foreign Relations, *Annual Report, 1992*, 14.
12. See the CFR study by Jessica Stern, *The Ultimate Terrorists* (Cambridge, Mass.: Harvard University Press, 1999).
13. *The Trilateral Commission at 25* (New York: The Trilateral Commission, 1998).
14. Quoted in *Newsweek*, 24 March 1980.
15. Trilateral Commission, "About the Trilateral Commission," 1998.
16. Council on Economic Development, "About the CED," 1999, 2.
17. Business Roundtable, "An Introduction to the Business Roundtable," 1999, 1.
18. Business Roundtable, "What the Roundtable Is," 1988, 1.
19. G. William Domhoff, *The Powers That Be* (New York: Random House, 1978), 61.

NOTES TO CHAPTER 4

1. *Buckley* v. *Valeo*, 424 U.S. 1 (1976).
2. See Frank J. Sorauf, *Inside Campaign Finance* (New Haven, Conn.: Yale University Press, 1992).

NOTES TO CHAPTER 5

1. Jeffrey M. Berry, *The New Liberalism: The Rising Power of Citizen Groups* (Washington, D.C.: Brookings Institution, 1999).
2. Jack L. Walker, *Mobilizing Interest Groups in American Politics* (Ann Arbor: University of Michigan Press, 1991).
3. *Fortune*, 8 December 1997.
4. Center for Responsive Politics, *Influence Inc.*, 1999.
5. C. Wright Mills, *The Power Elite* (New York: Oxford University Press, 1956), 289.
6. The political science literature is extensive but mixed in its findings regarding the effect of PAC contributions on congressional voting. See James B. Kau and Paul H. Rubin, *Congressmen, Constituents, and Contributors: Determinants of Roll Call Votes in the House of Representatives* (Boston: Martinus Nijhoff, 1982); J. Wright, "Contributions, Lobbying, and Committee Voting in the U.S. House of Representatives," *American Political Science Review* 84 (June 1999): 417–38; Janet M. Grezke, "PACs and the Congressional Supermarket: The Currency Is Complex," *American Journal of Political Science* 33 (1989): 1–24; F.L. Davis, "Balancing the Perspective on PAC Contributions: In Search of an Impact on Roll Calls," *American Politics Quarterly* 21 (April 1993): 205–22.

NOTES TO CHAPTER 6

1. William A. Henry, "News as Entertainment," in *What's News*, ed. Elie Abel (San Francisco: Institute for Contemporary Studies, 1981), 134.
2. E.E. Schattschneider, *The Semisovereign People* (New York: Holt, Rinehart & Winston, 1961), 68.

3. Bernard Cohen, *The Press and Foreign Policy* (Princeton: Princeton University Press, 1963), 10.

4. See Doris A. Graber, *Mass Media and American Politics,* 5th ed. (Washington, D.C.: CQ Press, 1996).

5. National Institute of Mental Health, *Television and Behavior* (Washington, D.C.: Government Printing Office, 1982).

6. Ted Smith, "The Watchdog's Bite," *American Enterprise* 2 (January/February 1990): 66.

7. Michael J. Robinson, "Public Affairs Television and the Growth of Political Malaise," *American Political Science Review* 70 (June 1976): 409–32. See also Thomas E. Patterson, *Out of Order* (New York: Random House, 1993).

8. See Austin Ranney, *Channels of Power* (New York: Basic Books, 1983).

9. Benjamin I. Page, Robert Y. Shapiro, and Glen R. Dempsey, "What Moves Public Opinion," *American Political Science Review* 81 (March 1987): 23–43.

NOTES TO CHAPTER 7

1. B. Guy Peters, *American Public Policy,* 5th ed. (New York: Chatham House, 1999), 73.

2. James Madison, *Federalist* No. 10.

3. Murray Edelman, *The Symbolic Uses of Politics* (Urbana: University of Illinois Press, 1964), 17.

4. "Speech to the Electors of Bristol," 3 November 1774.

5. Michael X. Delli Carpini and Scott Keeter, "The U.S. Public's Knowledge of Politics," *Public Opinion Quarterly* 55 (May 1991): 583–612.

6. Only 11 percent of respondents could remember how their U.S. representative had voted on *any* issue in the preceding two years. See Warren Miller et al., *American National Election Study 1990* (Ann Arbor, Mich.: Inter-University Consortium for Political Research, 1992), 126–29.

7. Richard F. Fenno, *Home Style: House Members in their Districts* (Boston: Little, Brown, 1978), 153; also quoted in Roger H. Davidson and Walter J. Oleszek, *Congress and Its Members* (Washington, D.C.: CQ Press, 2000), 149.

8. See John W. Kingdon, *Congressmen's Voting Decisions* (Chapel Hill: University of North Carolina Press, 1991).

9. Survey by Louis Harris, reported in *American Enterprise,* May/June, 1992, 103.

10. See Davidson and Oleszek, *Congress and Its Members.*

11. Alan Ehrenhalt, *The United States of Ambition: Politicians, Power, and the Pursuit of Office* (New York: Random House, 1991), 22.

12. See Frank Sorauf, *Inside Campaign Finance* (New Haven: Yale University Press, 1992).

13. Much anecdotal evidence is collected by Public Citizen. See that organization's publication *Campaign Finance Quid Pro Quos,* 25 March 1997.

14. Representative Romano Mazzolli (D-Ky.), as quoted in *Money Begets Access, Access Begets Action,* Center for Responsive Politics, 1999, 1.

15. Representative Mel Levine (D-Calif.), as quoted in Martin Schram, *Speaking Freely: Former Members of Congress Talk about Money and Politics,* Center for Responsive Politics, 1995, 89.

16. *Solicitation: None Dare Call It Coercion or Extortion,* Center for Responsive Politics, 1999, 1.

17. Ibid., 2.

18. See David Epstein and Peter Zemsky, "Money Talks: Deterring Quality Challengers in Congressional Elections," *American Political Science Review* 89 (June 1995): 295–308.

19. Peters, *American Public Policy,* 89.

NOTES TO CHAPTER 8

1. Donald S. Van Meter, "The Policy Implementation Process," *Administration and Society* 6 (February 1975): 447.

2. "Key Regulatory Facts and Figures," Regulation.org. Sponsored by the Heritage Foundation, Washington, D.C. See also Kenneth J. Meier, *Politics and the Bureaucracy* (Ft. Worth, Tex.: Harcourt Brace, 2000).

3. H.H. Gerth and C. Wright Mills, *From Max Weber* (New York: Oxford, 1958).
4. William Niskanen, *Bureaucracy and Representative Government* (Chicago: Aldine, 1971).
5. Aaron Wildavsky, *The New Politics of the Budgetary Process* (Glenview, Ill.: Scott, Foresman, 1988).
6. James Q. Wilson, *Bureaucracy: What Bureaucrats Do and Why They Do It* (New York: Basic Books, 1989).
7. Data available at the Office of the Federal Register. See also U.S. General Accounting Office, *Regulatory Reform Yields Mixed Results* (Washington, D.C.: GAO, 1997).
8. See Thomas D. Hopkins, *Regulatory Costs in Profile* (Washington, D.C.: Center for the Study of American Business, 1996).
9. Reginal S. Sheehan, "Federal Agencies and the Supreme Court," *American Politics Quarterly* 20 (October 1992): 478–500.

NOTES TO CHAPTER 9

1. General Accounting Office, *Federal Evaluation Issues* (Washington, D.C.: GAO, 1989), 4.
2. See, for example, David Nachmias, *Public Policy Evaluation* (New York: St. Martin's Press, 1979); Evert Vedung, *Public Policy and Program Evaluation* (New Brunswick, N.J.: Transaction, 1997).
3. Anne Schneider and Helen Ingram, "Social Construction of Target Populations: Implications for Politics and Policy," *American Political Science Review* 87 (June 1993): 334–47.
4. B. Guy Peters, *American Public Policy*, 5th ed. (New York: Chatham House, 1999), 175.
5. Ibid., 176–82.
6. Charles E. Lindblom and Edward J. Woodhouse, *The Policy-Making Process*, 3d ed. (Englewood Cliffs, N.J.: Prentice Hall, 1993), 31.
7. Charles E. Lindblom, *The Intelligence of Democracy: Decision Making through Mutual Adjustment* (New York: Free Press, 1965).

Index